SHREWSBURY TO CHESTER

Vic Mitchell and Keith Smith

MP Middleton Press

Front cover: Shrewsbury Castle is in the background of this 1957 panorama of the west end of the station. Suitably framed are no. 45501 St. Dunstan's *and no. 45644* Howe, *both ex-LMS 4-6-0s. (SLS coll.)*

Back cover: Entering Shrewsbury on 4th September 1981 is no. 33005 with the 08.01 Crewe to Cardiff train. It is passing under a duct carrying mailbags. (P.Jones)

Published February 2010

ISBN 978 1 906008 70 3

© Middleton Press, 2010

Design Deborah Esher

Published by
    Middleton Press
    Easebourne Lane
    Midhurst
    West Sussex
    GU29 9AZ
Tel: 01730 813169
Fax: 01730 812601
Email: info@middletonpress.co.uk
www.middletonpress.co.uk

Printed in the United Kingdom by Henry Ling Limited, at the Dorset Press, Dorchester, DT1 1HD

INDEX

ACKNOWLEDGEMENTS

We are very grateful for the assistance received from many of those mentioned in the credits also to B.Bennett, A.R.Carder, L.Crosier, G.Croughton, S.C.Jenkins, D.A.Johnson, N.Langridge, B.Lewis, D.H.Mitchell, D.J.Mitchell, A.C.Mott, P.Mottram, B.Robbins, D.T.Rowe, Mr D. and Dr S.Salter, E.Wilmshurst and in particular, our always supportive wives, Barbara Mitchell and Janet Smith.

I. The route diagram from 1947 has the GWR with bold lines. (GWR)

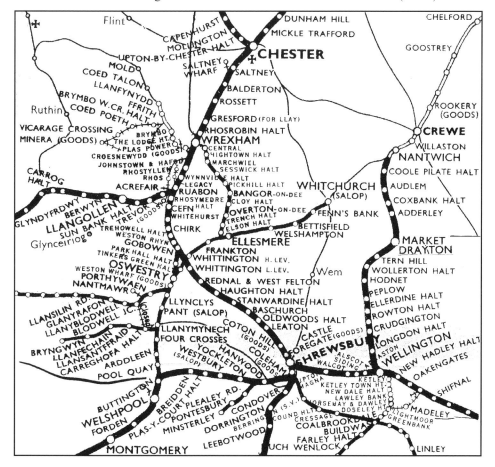

GEOGRAPHICAL SETTING

The county town of Shrewsbury evolved from an ancient settlement created on a high area within a horse-shoe loop in the River Severn. A northward tributary is the River Perry and our route passes over it south of Rednal & West Felton. The line was built on sandstone and marl in this district.

North of Gobowen, the line is close to or over coal deposits, which were mined until recent times. The final few miles are mostly on sandstone and a steady descent takes place into the flat Dee Valley surrounding the other county town of Chester.

The first part of the route was built in Shropshire, but the Chirk-Rossett section was constructed in Denbighshire and was thus in Wales. The final five miles were (and are) in Cheshire.

The maps are to the scale of 25ins to 1 mile, with north at the top unless otherwise stated. Welsh spelling and hyphenation has varied over the years and so we have generally used the most recent form, as have the railways.

II. Gradient profile

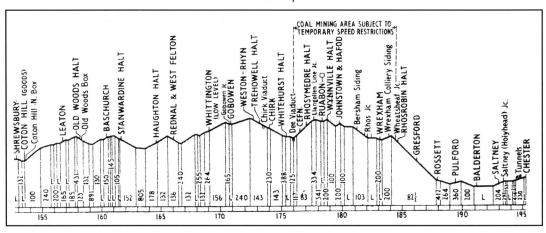

July 1910

HISTORICAL BACKGROUND

The Grand Junction Railway reached Chester from Crewe in 1840, the year in which the Chester & Birkenhead Railway was completed.

The Shrewsbury & Chester Railway opened on 4th November 1846, its southern temporary terminus being at Rhosymedre, just south of Cefn. The route was completed on 14th October 1848.

Shrewsbury was served by the Shrewsbury & Birmingham Railway from 1849, the Shrewsbury & Hereford Railway from 1858, the London & North Western Railway from Crewe from 1862, the Shrewsbury & Welshpool Railway from 1862, the Severn Valley Railway also from 1862 and the Potteries, Shrewsbury & North Wales Railway (actually just a local line westwards) from 1866. This was later known as the Shropshire & Montgomeryshire Railway.

Chester received the Chester & Holyhead Railway in 1848, the Birkenhead, Lancashire & Cheshire Junction Railway in 1850, the Cheshire Lines Committee trains from the east in 1874 and from the west came the Manchester, Sheffield & Lincolnshire Railway in 1890.

Wrexham had the Wrexham & Minera Railway from 1862, the Wrexham, Mold & Connah's Quay trains from the north from 1866 and the Wrexham & Ellesmere services from the south from 1895.

Between Wrexham and Ruabon, west of the main line, were the lines of the Shropshire Union Railways & Canal Company. Parts were in use between 1863 and 1963. Ruabon received trains from the Vale of Llangollen Railway from 1861, these running from Dolgelly from 1868.

Chirk had the benefit of the Glyn Valley Tramway from 1873 until 1935, but it was narrow gauge. The final branch on the route southwards was from Gobowen to Oswestry and this was opened by the S&CR in 1848. This branch and the entire main line became part of the Great Western Railway in 1854.

With the advent of nationalisation, all the GWR lines in the area became part of the Western Region of British Railways on 1st January 1948. The route was transferred to the London Midland Region on 17th June 1963 operationally, but officially on 1st January.

Privatisation resulted in Central Trains operating services from 2nd March 1997. However, after reorganisation in October 2001, Wales & Borders became the franchisee. Arriva Trains Wales took over in December 2003.

Closure dates of the branches, the intermediate stations and the goods depots are given in the captions.

PASSENGER SERVICES

We look at train frequencies in the down (northward) direction on weekdays and have the Sunday figure in brackets. Trains running on less than five days in a week are excluded.

The 1848 timetable showed 6 (3) trains. The figures were 7 (2) in 1854 and 10 (2) in 1869. North-to-West services began in 1888 and by 1899 there were 16 (2) trains, with several extras over short parts of the route, notably north of Ruabon, being shown in Bradshaw.

The 1929 service comprised 12 (4) through services, with an increase in local trains. The year 1959 offered 15 (8), but the next year brought cuts, with the closure of most intermediate stations. By 1966 the figures were 10 (6), but Bradshaw had ceased in 1962.

The sleeping cars to Birkenhead and other through trains from Paddington (except one) were withdrawn on 6th March 1967. The 1985 timetable offered 10 (6), calling at all stations, which was typical for around 30 years.

Bradshaw-Mitchell's *Rail Times* (Middleton Press) for July 2008 was the first to announce 6 (3) Wrexham & Shropshire trains from Marylebone to that town from that month. From December of that year Virgin Trains introduced an evening train from Euston via Chester, on Mondays to Fridays, to Wrexham.

BIRMINGHAM & SHREWSBURY and SHREWSBURY & CHESTER.

Geo. Knox, Sec. W. S. Darkin, Assist. Sec. Dudley Parsons, Traffic Manager.

From W'hampton. MI	H. Robertson, Eng.]	Week Days.								Sundays.		Fares frm W'hmptn			
	Bristol....dep.	..	..	..	..	..	8 0	11 0	..	..	..	..	..	..	..
	Gloucester. ,,	..	..	..	..	7 0	9 38	12 35	..	..	..	..	..	..	..
	Derby .... ,,	..	..	..	..	8 0	11 15	..	2 0	..	..	..	..	..	..
	London .. ,,	..	..	..	..	..	10 0	..	12 0	..	..	..	..	..	..
	ForStations between London and Wolverhampton, page 34; between Bristol and Glo'ster, page 59.			1 2 3 class.	1 &2 class.	1& 2 clss.	1 & 2 clss.	1 & 2 class.	1 & 2 gov.	1 2 3 class.	1 & 2 gov.	1st class	2nd class	Day Tickets 1 clss	2 clss
				morn	morn	mrn	aft.	aft.	aft.	morn	aft.	s. d.	s. d.	s. d.	s. d.
—	**Birminghm** L.&N.W. dep	..	..	6 15	..	10 0	1 50	3 0	5 0	..	..	..	..	..	..
4½	**Wolvrhmptn**	..	..	7 10	10 20	1240	2 40	5 10	7 30	8 30	4 45	..	..	..	..
7½	Codsal	..	..	7 20	10 30	1250	2 50	5 20	7 40	8 44	4 55	0 10	0 8	1 3	1 0
12¼	Albrighton	..	..	7 30	10 40	1 0	3 0	5 30	7 50	8 54	5 5	1 4	1 0	2 0	1 6
16¼	**Shiffnall**	..	..	7 40	10 50	1 10	3 10	5 40	8 5	9 8	5 20	2 2	1 8	3 3	2 6
19¼	Oakengates	..	..	7 55	11 5	1 25	3 25	5 55	8 20	9 23	5 35	2 8	2 0	4 0	3 0
23¼	**Wellington**..	..	..	8 5	11 15	1 35	3 35	6 5	8 30	9 30	5 43	2 0	1 6	..	..
25¾	Walcot	..	..	8 15	11 25	1 45	3 45	6 15	8 40	9 44	5 55	3 10	2 11	..	..
29¼	Upton Magna ..	..	..	8 25	11 35	1 55	3 55	6 25	8 50	9 50	6 5	4 4	3 3	..	..
	Shrewsbry arr	..	..	8 40	11 50	2 10	4 5	6 40	9 0	10 0	6 15	3 0	2 6	4 6	3 9
Fm Salop	For trains from Shrewsbury to Newport and Stafford, page 57.	1 2 3 class	1 & 2 class	1 & 2 class	1 & 2 * *	1&2 clss.	1 & 2 class	1 2 3 class		1 2 3 class	1 2 3 class	Fares from Shrewsbury.			
		morn	morn	morn	noon	aft.	aft.	aft.		morn	aft.				
	Shrewsbry d	3 30	..	8 45	12 0	2 15	4 10	6 40	Llangollen to Corwen, Bala and Barmouth, by Coach, see page 111.	7 5	6 20	..	..	..	..
3¾	Leaton	..	..	8 53	12 10	2 25	..	6 49		7 15	6 25	0 10	0 8	..	..
7½	‖Baschurch	4 0	..	9 1	12 19	2 35	4 28	6 58		7 25	6 35	1 8	1 4	2 6	2 0
13	§Rednal	4 20	..	9 11	12 32	2 49	4 40	7 8		7 39	6 49	2 10	2 2	..	..
16	‡Whittington ..	4 34	..	9 16	12 39	2 55	4 47	7 16		7 48	7 0	3 5	2 8	5 2	4 0
18	†Gobowen	4 43	7 42	9 20	12 45	3 0	4 53	7 22		7 55	7 5	3 11	3 0	6 0	4 6
20¼	**Oswstry** a	..	..	9 35	12 55	3 15	5 5	7 37		8 10	7 20	4 2	3 0	6 3	4 6
	,, d	..	7 35	9 0	12 35	2 45	4 45	7 10		7 40	6 50	6 0	4 4	9 0	6 6
19¾	Presgwyn	4 51	7 47	..	12 51	3 7	..	7 28		8 1	7 11	4 4	3 3	..	..
20¾	**Chirk**........	4 59	7 51	9 30	12 55	3 12	5 0	7 33		8 6	7 16	4 7	3 6	7 0	5 3
22¼	***Llangolln R.**	5 7	7 56	9 35	1 0	3 18	5 4	7 38		8 12	7 22	4 11	3 8	7 6	5 6
23¼	Cefn	..	8 1	9 40	..	3 24	..	7 43		8 17	7 27	5 2	3 10	..	..
24¾	**Rhuabon**....	5 29	8 8	9 47	1 10	3 34	5 14	7 49		8 24	7 34	5 4	4 2	..	..
27	Rhos	5 38	8 14	..	1 16	3 41	..	7 56		8 30	7 40	5 10	4 5	..	..
30	**Wrexham** ..	5 56	8 20	9 57	1 22	3 59	5 25	8 4		8 39	7 49	6 5	4 10	9 6	7 6
33	Gresford	..	8 28	10 4	1 29	3 57	5 32	8 12		8 48	7 58	7 1	5 3	..	..
34¾	Rossett........	6 17	8 33	10 9	1 34	4 2	5 38	8 17		8 54	8 4	7 4	5 5	..	..
36¼	Pulford........	6 24	8 38	..	1 39	4 8	..	8 23		9 0	8 10	7 8	5 8	..	..
39½	Saltney........	6 40	8 47	10 19	1 49	4 19	5 49	8 33		9 10	8 20	8 6	6 4	..	..
42½	**Chester** ..arr	6 50	8 55	10 25	1 55	4 25	5 55	8 40		9 15	8 30	9 0	7 0	13 6	10 6
	ForStations between Chester and Bangor, page 44; between Chester and Birkenhead page 56.	1 & 2 class.	1 & 2 exp.	1 & 2 class.	class.	1 &2 exp.	1 & 2 class.	1 2 3 class.		1 2 3 class.	1 2 3 class.				
		morn	morn	noon	aft.	aft.	aft.	aft.		morn	aft.				
42	**Chester** dep.	8 30	9 0	12 0	2 0	4 45	6 0	8 45		9 30	8 45	..	..	..	..
99½	**Bangor** arr	12 15	12 55	..	..	..	..	12 10		8 30	..	21 6	16 9	24 0	18 0
57	Birkenhead ,,	9 15	9 30	12 45	2 45	5 25	6 45	9 30		10 15	9 30	11 6	9 0	18 6	14 6
58	Liverpool.. ,,	9 35	9 45	1 5	3 5	5 40	7 5	9 50		10 35	9 50	11 8	9 2	..	..
84	Manchester ,,	12 30	12 45	..	..	..	..	..		..	..	17 2	13 2	..	..

DAY TICKETS issued on Saturday to return on the Sunday or Monday following. Day tickets not transferable, and to return the same day by any train, will be issued to and from all the principal stations. Gov. fares, one penny per mile. * * 1st, 2nd, and 3rd class from Rhuabon. Season tickets, per mile, 1st class—12 months, 20s.; 6 months, 12s.; 3 months, 8s. 2nd class, 15s.; 6 months, 9s.; 3 months, 6s.

March 1850

➔ III. The map is at 20ins to 1 mile and is from 1927. The S&CR established its locomotive depot on the left, the building eventually being occupied by the road vehicles of National Carriers. It now houses luxury apartments. The main line to Chester is top left, while the route to Crewe is top right. Between the two is Castle Foregate goods yard and the BP oil depot. The yard functioned into the late 1980s. Its crane is marked; this was rated at 6-tons. The continuation south and the illustrations of that area appear in the albums listed near picture no. 7.

SHREWSBURY

WOOD STREET WOOD STREET

Saw Mill

Wood Street
Gardens

Allotment
Gardens

Oil Depot

Castle Mall

DERFALD STREET

Old
School

Infant
Sch

DERFALD
SQUARE

Probable Site of
Catherines Chapel

G.P.
Inn

Crane

P.H.

JANES PLACE

Infant
School

Landing
Stage

Goods Shed

Goods
Shed

Perseverance
Iron Works

A
CASTLE
FIELDS
WARD
(Det.)

Corn
Mill

Goods Shed

Ward Bay

Congl. Church

CHESTER STREET

CASTLE FOREGATE

Britannia Place

HALL'S PASSAGE

Postal
Sorting
Office

School

BEACALLS LANE

WHARF ROAD

Urinal

CHESTER STREET

HOWARD STREET

HIS MAJESTY'S
PRISON

Staff		
	Passenger	Goods
1913	157	59
1929	186	66
1937	157	96

1.   The station was used by three companies in the early years and was termed "United". After it came under GWR control, the suffix "General" was applied and extra platforms were added in 1861-63. To improve access to them, the ground was lowered in front of the main building in about 1900 and a new entrance was made into the former basement. A fresh booking office was provided at this level and a subway was built to the platforms. The ground on the right was cut away, as was part of the foot of the castle mound. It seems that the doors and windows had been provided, ready. (A.Dudman coll.)

2.   An overall roof was built in the mid-1860s, but the northern part of it was removed in 1924 and not 1931-32, as often stated. The southern section lasted until 1961-62 and is seen shortly before its demolition, along with no. 5324, a 4300 class 2-6-0. (Ted Hancock Railway Photographs)

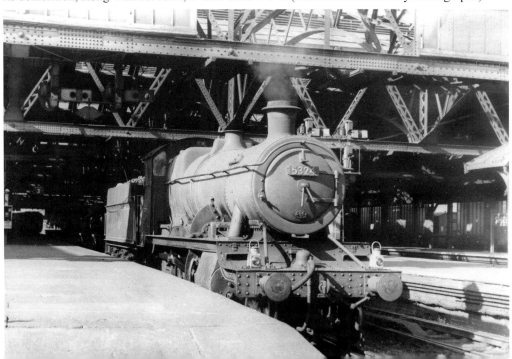

3.   Crewe Junction signal box is largely obscured by the locomotive of an express bound for Birkenhead. On the bridge over Castle Foregate is no. 6868 *Penrhos Grange* on 27th April 1963. The platforms had been renumbered in 1950 and electric lighting was completed in 1964. The box of 1903 was fitted with a 120-lever frame and was still in use more than 100 years later. (A.M.Davies)

4.   In the background is the castle and also the footbridge known as The Dana. It carries a public footpath to the prison and once had steps to the platforms. Another footbridge linking the platforms was at their south end until 1961. This southward view along platform 4 is from 31st September 1976. (D.A.Thompson)

5.   "The train standing at platform 2 is from Devil's Bridge". This was true on 10th March 1978. The coach was off its bogies and standing on a long wagon, while undergoing maintenance. This winter custom had been practised for around ten years. (C.C.Green)

> **Other albums which include coverage of the station, engine sheds and goods yards are *Kidderminster to Shrewsbury, Shrewsbury to Ludlow, Shrewsbury to Newtown* and *Wolverhampton to Shrewsbury*. The S&MR is featured in *Branch Line to Shrewsbury*.**

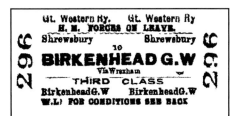

6.   Comparison with the front cover photograph will reveal the changes in the signalling. On the left is part of the bridgework erected to accommodate the mailbag conveyor system and removed in 2004. Major renovation work took place in the early 1980s. A three-car class 120 'Cross-country' unit forms the 1615 departure from Shrewsbury to Crewe on 10th August 1982. (P.Shannon)

7.   Standing at platform 3 on 26th June 2008 is no. 67025 *Western Star* with the 10.17 from Marylebone to Wrexham General. The platform could accommodate 13 coaches, but there were only four in this train. Between 1967 and 1990, there were no London trains, apart from some on Summer Saturdays, from here. Platform 3 had been little used for many years. (V.Mitchell)

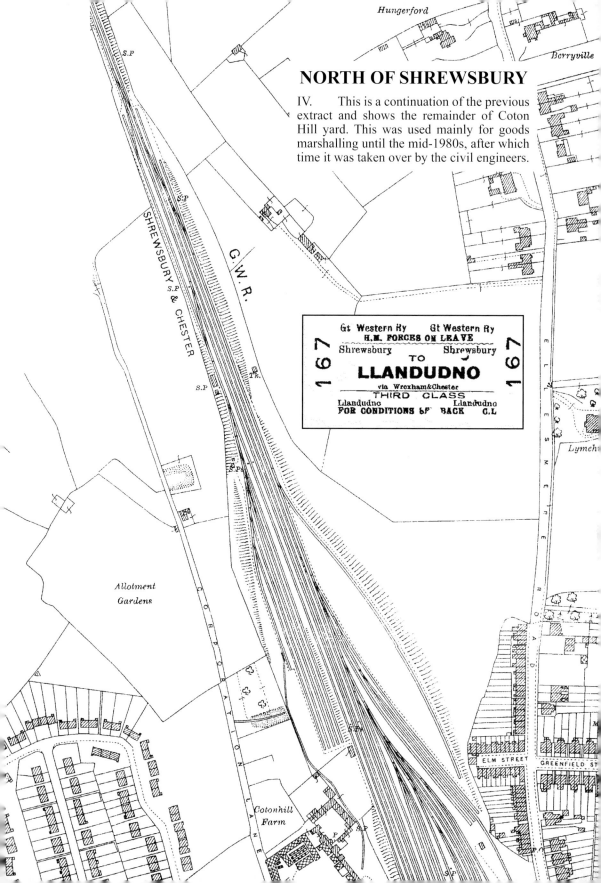

Hungerford

Bcrryville

NORTH OF SHREWSBURY

IV.   This is a continuation of the previous extract and shows the remainder of Coton Hill yard. This was used mainly for goods marshalling until the mid-1980s, after which time it was taken over by the civil engineers.

S.P

SHREWSBURY & CHESTER

S.P

S.P

S.P

G.W.R.

S.P

T.K.

S.P

S.Ps

Allotment
Gardens

167
Gt Western Ry   Gt Western Ry
H.M. FORCES ON LEAVE
Shrewsbury   Shrewsbury
TO
LLANDUDNO
via Wrexham&Chester
THIRD CLASS
Llandudno   Llandudno
FOR CONDITIONS SF BACK   C.L
167

Lymch

ELLESMERE ROAD

ELM STREET

GREENFIELD ST

Cotonhill
Farm

8. There were two signal boxes: Coton Hill South (50 levers) which closed in 1972 and North (40 levers) which lasted until 1977. The latter is seen and was converted to a dwelling; it still stands. It had earlier had its superstructure destroyed by fire and a new frame came into use on 25th October 1955. South Box was demolished on 11th January 1964 by no. D1734, while it was hauling loaded cattle wagons and tanks of ammonia. The signalman died. (F.Giddins)

9. No. 7922 *Salford Hall* is arriving with an express from Birkenhead, in about 1960. The goods office and the line to Crewe are on the right. (J.A.G.H.Coltas coll.)

10.   The prison is prominent in the background of this panorama of Coton Hill yard on 23rd April 1977. No. 6000 *King George V* is working a special to Chester from Hereford, where it was based at that time. Such trips began in 1972. It was the locomotives 50th anniversary run and Severn Valley coaches were used. (T.Heavyside)

11.   The S&CR's engine shed was on the left, but the GWR concentrated locomotive accommodation south of the station, at Coleham. The S&CR's first station was within this view and was closed on 1st June 1849, when "United" was available. No. 47108 approaches the station with train 6G29, the 14.46 Penyffordd to Oakengates cement train, on 10th August 1982. The train consists of vacuum-braked Presflo wagons, which would soon be replaced by air-braked stock. (P.Shannon)

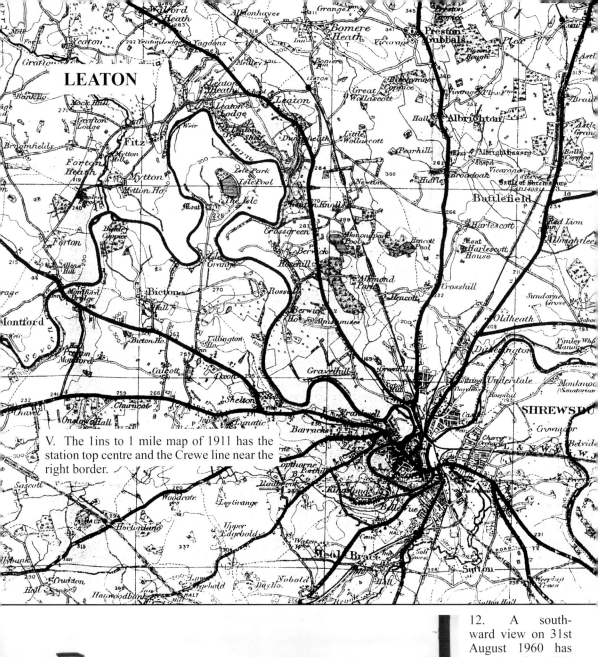

LEATON

V. The 1ins to 1 mile map of 1911 has the station top centre and the Crewe line near the right border.

12. A south-ward view on 31st August 1960 has vans in the 1909 goods yard in the right background. The down waiting shelter appears to have been designed as a place for prayer meetings. There was a staff of six in the 1930s. (R.G.Nelson/ T.Walsh)

13.   More splendid barge boards were recorded on 12th September 1960, along with the 1905 signal box, which had 21 levers and closed on 12th November 1987. The gates were replaced by automatic half barriers and the box was moved to Glyndyfrydwy on the Llangollen Railway. (P.J.Garland/R.S.Carpenter)

14.   The station closed to passengers on 12th September 1960 and to goods on 15th March 1965. Two class 7800 2-6-0s are working an Oswestry to Shrewsbury freight on 30th August 1966. (H.Ballantyne)

Leaton	1903	1913	1923	1933
Passenger tickets issued	13393	12419	10623	5366
Season tickets issued	*	*	100	18
Parcels forwarded	3354	8708	10263	1037
General goods forwarded (tons)		72	68	28
Coal and coke received (tons)	Opened for	-	356.	339
Other minerals received (tons)	Goods	2978	319	62
General goods received (tons)	Traffic	1005	1080	151
Coal and Coke handled	in 1909	683	810	631
Trucks of livestock handled		25	17	12

BASCHURCH

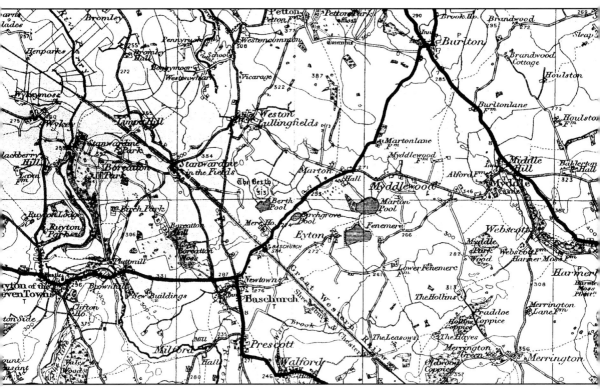

VI.   The 1911 edition at 1ins to 1 mile reveals that the station was a long walk from the village. This was soon to have an adequate bus service from its centre. A halt called Oldwoods was near the bottom of the map from 3rd July 1933. A siding nearby was in use until 6th April 1964. North of Baschurch was Stanwardine Halt (opened 27th February 1933) and Haughton Halt (opened 22nd September 1934). All three closed on 12th September 1960, but Haughton sidings were in use until 6th March 1994.

15.   A southward panorama on 31st August 1960 includes the lamp room (left). It was always remote from other buildings for safety reasons. There were 11 to 13 men here in the period 1913-38. (R.G.Nelson/T.Walsh)

16. This is the scene on 14th February 1961 after the 7.35pm Wellington to Chester hit a bogie bolster wagon in a long train being reversed into the siding by a 2-8-0. The six coaches were running at 40-45mph behind no. 6949 *Habberfield Hall*. Its crew and one other railwayman died; the signalman was to blame. (R.S.Carpenter)

Baschurch	1903	1913	1923	1933
Passenger tickets issued	27826	29351	21009	14865
Season tickets issued	*	*	98	32
Parcels forwarded	14535	35200	57571	88261
General goods forwarded (tons)	1182	1717	2190	361
Coal and coke received (tons)	4439	3528	2557	2387
Other minerals received (tons)	5284	7250	3745	1939
General goods received (tons)	6508	6588	5379	2206
Coal and Coke handled	3715	4066	3827	4453
Trucks of livestock handled	451	585	391	242

17.   There was a staff of 11 or 12 in the period 1913-38. This view from the same period includes the wreckage, plus no. 2866, a 2-8-0 of the 2800 class. (Stations UK)

18.   The population was recorded as 1457 in 1901. The goods yard closed on 5th July 1965 and it was shown to have a 3-ton capacity crane in 1938. The photograph is from 28th July 1984. The elegant building on the left is the pump house. (Ted Hancock Railway Photographs)

19.   The box had 25 levers from 1911 and was in use until 28th March 1999. This is the 12.22 Crewe to Shrewsbury via Chester on 9th May 1989. The DMU is no. 150140. The 1900 box had 29 levers. (P.G.Barnes)

20.   Passenger service ceased here on 12th September 1960, but the building could still be admired in May 2002, along with its tasteful extension. A class 60 is southbound with steel in May 2002. (S.R.Dewey)

REDNAL & WEST FELTON

VII.   The map is almost continuous from the previous one and has the station at the bottom. The route of the Cambrian Railways is from top right to lower left.

21.   A southward view in November 1959 includes the 29-lever signal box, which lasted until 1963. The suffix was added on 16th October 1907, but a footbridge never was. (A.M.Davies)

22.   The opposite direction was recorded on the same day. There were eight men listed here throughout the 1930s. Passenger service ceased on 12th September 1960. (A.M.Davies)

23.   The goods yard was photographed on 3rd October 1963; it closed four days later. There was a three-ton capacity crane provided. (P.J.Garland/R.S.Carpenter)

Rednal and West Felton	1903	1913	1923	1933
Passenger tickets issued	9990	10033	7049	2855
Season tickets issued	*	*	-	4
Parcels forwarded	8460	7269	5169	1773
General goods forwarded (tons)	1229	1553	885	624
Coal and coke received (tons)	2365	1562	724	530
Other minerals received (tons)	499	461	581	1639
General goods received (tons)	1138	786	1468	2163
Coal and Coke handled	474	434	960	965
Trucks of livestock handled	31	25	88	29

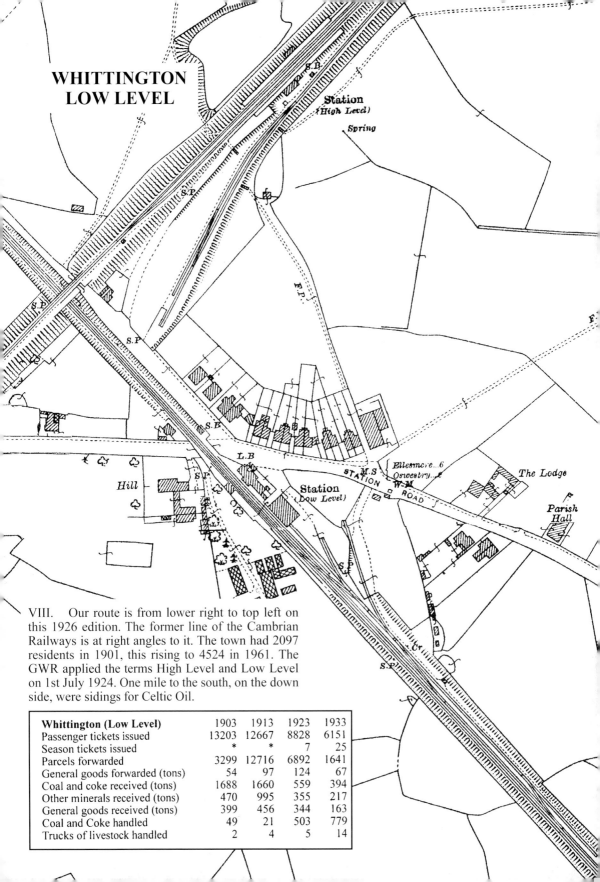

WHITTINGTON
LOW LEVEL

VIII.   Our route is from lower right to top left on this 1926 edition. The former line of the Cambrian Railways is at right angles to it. The town had 2097 residents in 1901, this rising to 4524 in 1961. The GWR applied the terms High Level and Low Level on 1st July 1924. One mile to the south, on the down side, were sidings for Celtic Oil.

Whittington (Low Level)	1903	1913	1923	1933
Passenger tickets issued	13203	12667	8828	6151
Season tickets issued	*	*	7	25
Parcels forwarded	3299	12716	6892	1641
General goods forwarded (tons)	54	97	124	67
Coal and coke received (tons)	1688	1660	559	394
Other minerals received (tons)	470	995	355	217
General goods received (tons)	399	456	344	163
Coal and Coke handled	49	21	503	779
Trucks of livestock handled	2	4	5	14

24.   This eastward view from the 1950s reveals the extent to which the platform has been raised in a century, as the doorways are down behind railings. There were five or six employees here during the 1930s. (Lens of Sutton coll.)

25.   The goods shed provided additional shelter for the up platform. Passenger services ceased on 12th September 1960 and goods ended on 7th October 1963. The former applied to the High Level on 7th January 1960. (Ted Hancock Railway Photographs)

26.   On the right is the road to High Level and the bridge carrying trains to it. The signal box had a 20-lever frame from 1912 and closed on 14th March 1992. Automatic half barriers replaced the gates. (P.J.Garland/R.S.Carpenter)

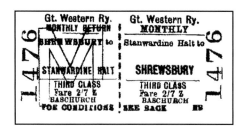

Gt. Western Ry.
MONTHLY RETURN

SHREWSBURY to

STANWARDINE HALT

THIRD CLASS
Fare 2/7 ½
BASCHURCH
FOR CONDITIONS

Gt. Western Ry.
MONTHLY

Stanwardine Halt to

SHREWSBURY

THIRD CLASS
Fare 2/7 ½
BASCHURCH
SEE BACK

1476

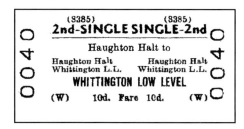

(8385)   (8385)
2nd-SINGLE SINGLE-2nd

Haughton Halt to

Haughton Halt   Haughton Halt
Whittington L.L.   Whittington L.L.

WHITTINGTON LOW LEVEL

(W)   10d. Fare 10d.   (W)

0040

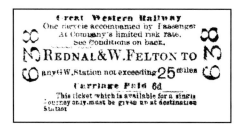

Great Western Railway
One bicycle accompanied by Passenger
At Company's limited risk rate.
See Conditions on back.

REDNAL & W. FELTON TO

any G.W. Station not exceeding 25 miles

Carriage Paid 6d

This ticket which is available for a single
journey only must be given up at destination
Station

638

2nd · SINGLE   SINGLE · 2nd

Rednal & West Felton to
Rednal&W.Felton   Rednal&W.Felton

Whittington L.L.   Whittington L.L.

WHITTINGTON L.L

(W)   8d   Fare   8d   (W)

For conditions see over For conditions see over

509

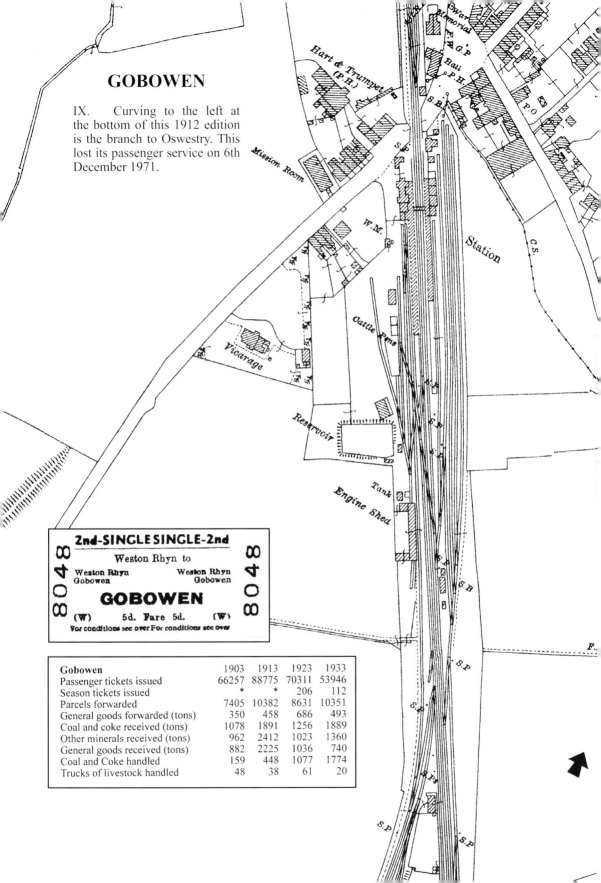

GOBOWEN

IX.   Curving to the left at the bottom of this 1912 edition is the branch to Oswestry. This lost its passenger service on 6th December 1971.

Hart & Trumpet (P.H.)

Mission Room

W.M.

Vicarage

Reservoir

Cattle Pens

Station

Tank

Engine Shed

War Memorial

G.P.

Hall P.H.

S.B.

P.O.

C.S.

S.P.

S.B.

S.P.

S.P.

S.P.

S.P.

F.

Gobowen	1903	1913	1923	1933
Passenger tickets issued	66257	88775	70311	53946
Season tickets issued	*	*	206	112
Parcels forwarded	7405	10382	8631	10351
General goods forwarded (tons)	350	458	686	493
Coal and coke received (tons)	1078	1891	1256	1889
Other minerals received (tons)	962	2412	1023	1360
General goods received (tons)	882	2225	1036	740
Coal and Coke handled	159	448	1077	1774
Trucks of livestock handled	48	38	61	20

27.   Although Gobowen had a small population, the S&CR wanted to make an impression at its only junction. Could they do more? (Lens of Sutton coll.)

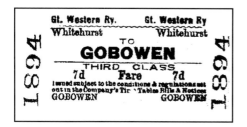

28.	Turning round, the traveller with architectural appreciation would be confronted with the Hart & Trumpet. The signal box was termed "North" and was completed in 1882.
(Lens of Sutton coll.)

29.	The up sidings are just visible in this photograph from about 1904 of a railmotor arriving, before the canopy was extended. The staff numbered 28 in 1923 and 23 in 1932. (Stations UK)

30. Class 8F 2-8-0 no. 48325 came to grief in about 1955. (F.Giddins)

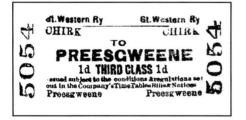

31.   A photograph from 14th September 1956 includes the branch autocoach for Oswestry, North Box and some of the up sidings, right. On the left is the run-round loop. (R.M.Casserley)

32.   Seen on 31st March 1962 is the weighbridge and its office (left), together with part of the goods yard, which closed on 2nd November 1964. There was a crane to lift only two tons. The yard reopened as a coal concentration depot in 1971 and was used by a coal merchant until 2007. (J.Langford)

33.   An up train departs towards London on 4th March 1967, hauled by no. 45132, an ex-LMS class 5 4-6-0. This was the last day of steam operation of the route. The Oswestry lines curve to the right. The nearest track gave branch trains direct access to the bay platform. The 18 miles to Shrewsbury were covered in 18 minutes, then the fastest steam in Britain. (A.M.Davies)

34.   South Box was built in 1882 and had an 80-lever frame fitted in 1911. Closure came on 5th June 1987, after which time the mineral-only Oswestry branch was little used until its closure in 1992. A ground frame was provided for access to it. No. 31226 awaits permission to proceed onto the branch at Gobowen South on 22nd August 1985, forming the then daily train of ballast hoppers to Blodwell. (P.Shannon)

35. No. 158766 waits to leave for Birmingham New Street in 1994 and we can examine the superbly restored main building. Ironically, the ticket office and waiting room were in the former crossing keepers cottage at the side of the road. (S.R.Dewey)

Other pictures of this station can be seen in our *Branch Lines around Oswestry*. They are nos 1 to 6.

36. A view from the train from Marylebone seen in picture 7 includes the signal box, which was still controlling some semaphore signals. The up platform was lengthened in 1914 and the canopy on the right probably dates from that time. (V.Mitchell)

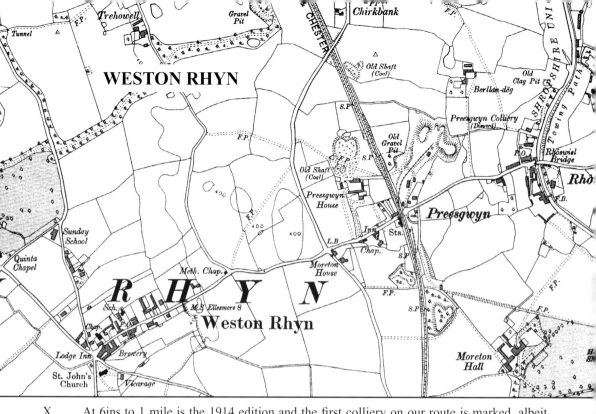

X.   At 6ins to 1 mile is the 1914 edition and the first colliery on our route is marked, albeit closed. The hall (lower right) became a school and some of its pupils operated the Gobowen booking office after privatisation.

37.   A northward view in 1950 includes part of the former colliery siding on the right and a goods loop on the left. There were nine employees here in the 1930s. The name was Preesgwyn for Weston Rhyn until February 1935; the station opened in November 1871. (Stations UK)

38.   A southward panorama from the signal box in about 1958 includes part of the goods yard, which was in use until 4th November 1963. The locomotive is no. 6956 *Mottram Hall*. One glass in the lamp is red, as a warning to road users that there is a level crossing. (Stations UK)

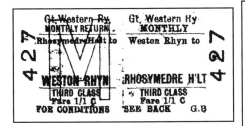

Weston Rhyn	1903	1913	1923	1933
Passenger tickets issued	17364	33477	32234	31263
Season tickets issued	*	*	109	97
Parcels forwarded	4869	19743	23831	19708
General goods forwarded (tons)	273	312	130	117
Coal and coke received (tons)	2552	3518	767	15
Other minerals received (tons)	4088	1451	10584	525
General goods received (tons)	2459	2042	5110	6137
Coal and Coke handled	40	126	128	20078
Trucks of livestock handled	-	-	-	-

39.   Ifton Colliery siding is on the right and some of the many rods control the loop on the left. The ringed signal is for the up loop. This and the next view date from October 1963. (P.J.Garland/R.S.Carpenter)

40.   The signal box was extended in 1924 and had 47 levers until closure on 3rd August 1991. Passenger service ceased on 12th September 1960. (P.J.Garland/R.S.Carpenter)

41.　　Stunning scenery is to be enjoyed in this district. Chirk Aqueduct is 418yds in length and it carries the Shropshire Union Canal across the Ceiriog Valley. No. 6000 *King George V* speeds north with a Hereford to Chester special on 26th April 1975 and enters Wales here. (T.Heavyside)

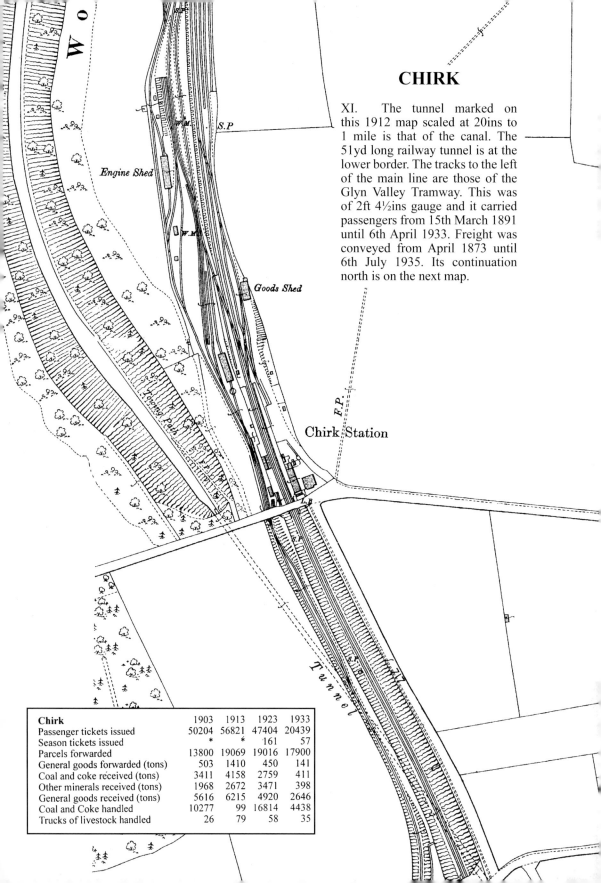

CHIRK

XI. The tunnel marked on this 1912 map scaled at 20ins to 1 mile is that of the canal. The 51yd long railway tunnel is at the lower border. The tracks to the left of the main line are those of the Glyn Valley Tramway. This was of 2ft 4½ins gauge and it carried passengers from 15th March 1891 until 6th April 1933. Freight was conveyed from April 1873 until 6th July 1935. Its continuation north is on the next map.

Engine Shed

Goods Shed

Chirk Station

Chirk	1903	1913	1923	1933
Passenger tickets issued	50204	56821	47404	20439
Season tickets issued	*	*	161	57
Parcels forwarded	13800	19069	19016	17900
General goods forwarded (tons)	503	1410	450	141
Coal and coke received (tons)	3411	4158	2759	411
Other minerals received (tons)	1968	2672	3471	398
General goods received (tons)	5616	6215	4920	2646
Coal and Coke handled	10277	99	16814	4438
Trucks of livestock handled	26	79	58	35

42.   A northward view from about 1910 includes the GWR goods shed and the 1874 signal box, ⁓ which had only 19 levers. (Stations UK)

43.   Looking south, we note the lack of a footbridge; there were steps down from the road. The local population was only 2611 in 1901 and 3652 in 1961. (Stations UK)

44.   A northward panorama from the road bridge on 31st October 1931 features details of the GVT, notably its engine shed. Its freight-only line continued into the distance for about half a mile. (R.S.Carpenter coll.)

45.   A canopy was added over the up platform in the early part of the 20th century. The goods yard closed on 13th July 1964 and the station became unstaffed on 1st April 1974; it was demolished in 1987. The locomotive in this 1960s view is 4-6-0 no. 44779. (SLS coll.)

46.   A Derby class 108 DMU calls with an up train on 26th September 1987. The Cadbury's siding in the background was disused at that time, but would be restored to use in late 1988 to provide access to Kronospan's siding. (P.Shannon)

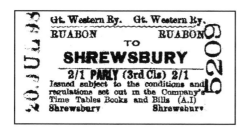

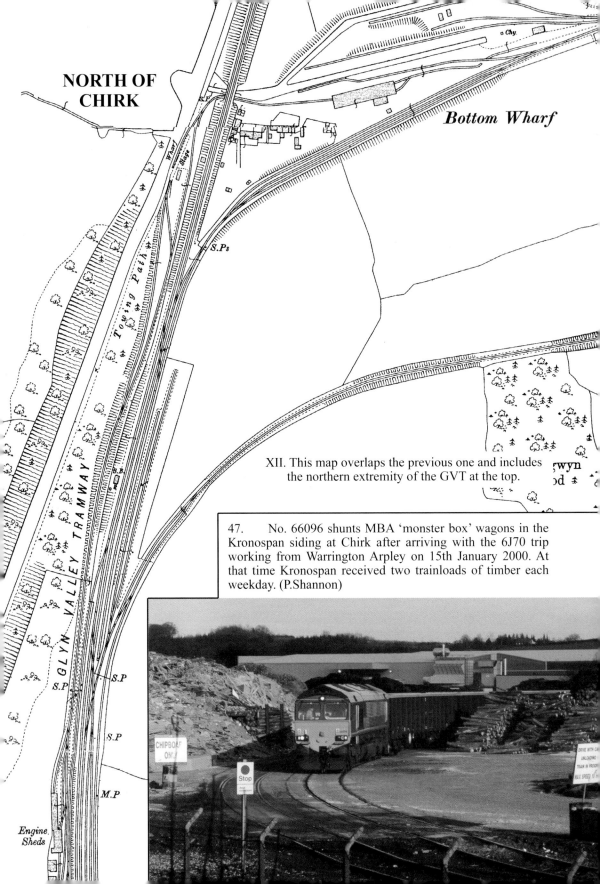

NORTH OF CHIRK

Bottom Wharf

R.P.

Wharf Stage

S.Ps

Towing Path

"GLYN VALLEY TRAMWAY"

S.B.

XII. This map overlaps the previous one and includes
the northern extremity of the GVT at the top.

rwyn
od

S.P

S.P

S.P

M.P

Engine
Sheds

47. No. 66096 shunts MBA 'monster box' wagons in the
Kronospan siding at Chirk after arriving with the 6J70 trip
working from Warrington Arpley on 15th January 2000. At
that time Kronospan received two trainloads of timber each
weekday. (P.Shannon)

CHIPBOARD
ONLY

Stop

DRIVE WITH CA
UNLOADING
TRAIN IN PROG
MAX SPEED 1

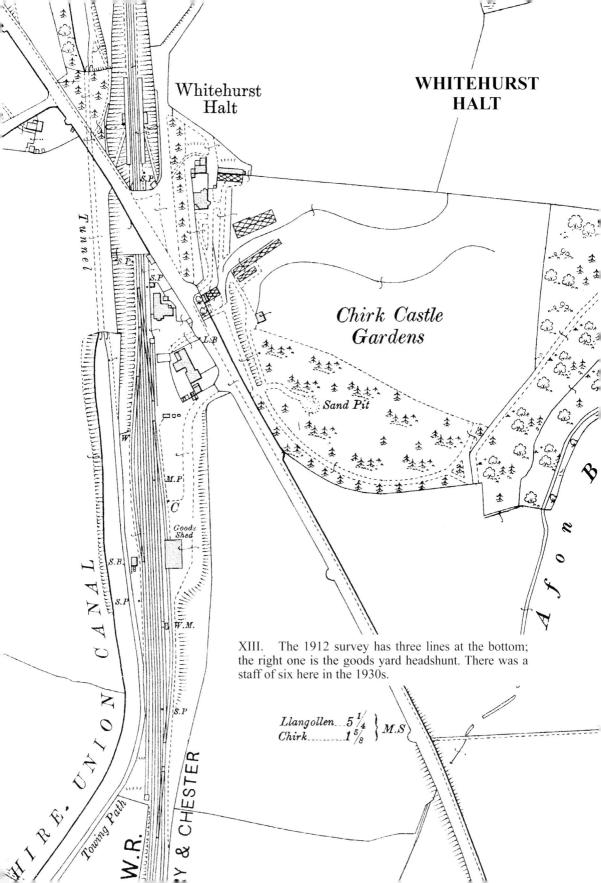

Whitehurst
Halt

**WHITEHURST
HALT**

*Chirk Castle
Gardens*

Sand Pit

Tunnel

S.P.

S.P.

S.P.

L.B

W

M.P

C

Goods
Shed

S.B.

S.P.

W.M.

S.P.

Towing Path

HIRE UNION CANAL

W.R.

Y & CHESTER

Afon B

XIII. The 1912 survey has three lines at the bottom;
the right one is the goods yard headshunt. There was a
staff of six here in the 1930s.

Llangollen....5$\frac{1}{4}$ } M.S
Chirk..........1$\frac{5}{8}$

48.　　A station opened as Llangollen Road south of the bridge on 14th October 1848 and closed on 1st July 1862, shortly after the Llangollen branch opened. This building is outlined on the map. The picture was taken in 1965; the signal box had been in the centre distance until 2nd February 1964. It had 27 levers. (P.J.Garland/R.S.Carpenter)

49.　　A halt opened north of the bridge on 1st October 1905 and was called Llangollen Road Halt until 1st May 1906, when it became Whitehurst Halt. It was known as Whitehurst Platform at different periods and closed as Whitehurst Halt on 12th September 1960. The photograph is from 1950; Fron Sidings signal box had been further north until 1947. (Stations UK)

SOUTH OF CEFN

50.   Cefn Viaduct is 418yds in length and passes over the River Dee. A little to the south of it is Whitehurst Tunnel, which is 46yds long. The river is in the foreground having meandered greatly. South of the viaduct was Froncysyllte Siding on the west side and a siding to a brick and tile works on the east. (P.J.Kelley)

Whitehurst	1903	1913	1923	1933
Passenger tickets issued	Opened	12829	4468	6832
Season tickets issued	for	*	20	39
Parcels forwarded	Goods Traffic in 1909	1660	1177	693
General goods forwarded (tons)	2490	1328	1045	904
Coal and coke received (tons)	20527	16451	9598	10946
Other minerals received (tons)	985	1144	1298	443
General goods received (tons)	1757	1336	1017	318
Coal and Coke handled	-	-	2951	782
Trucks of livestock handled	4	53	48	30

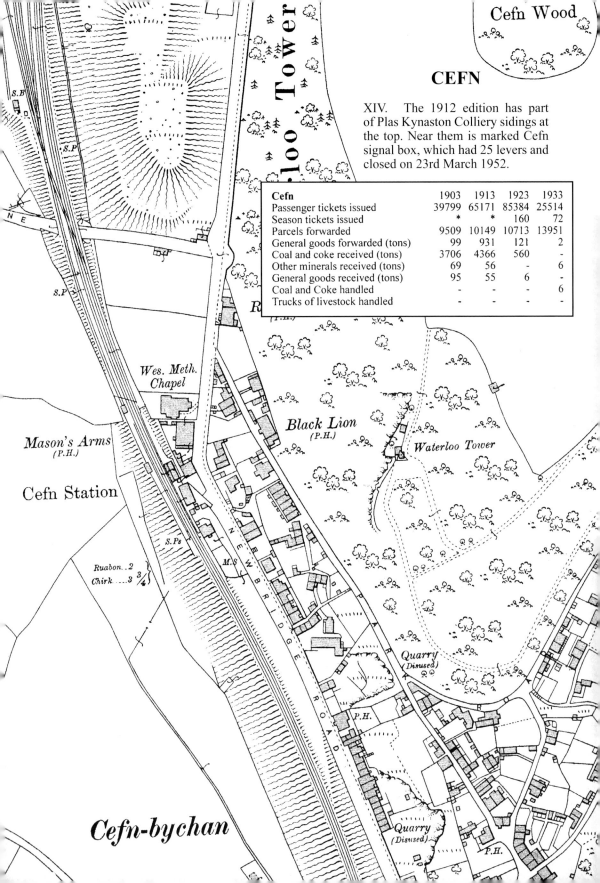

Cefn Wood

CEFN

XIV. The 1912 edition has part of Plas Kynaston Colliery sidings at the top. Near them is marked Cefn signal box, which had 25 levers and closed on 23rd March 1952.

Cefn	1903	1913	1923	1933
Passenger tickets issued	39799	65171	85384	25514
Season tickets issued	*	*	160	72
Parcels forwarded	9509	10149	10713	13951
General goods forwarded (tons)	99	931	121	2
Coal and coke received (tons)	3706	4366	560	-
Other minerals received (tons)	69	56	-	6
General goods received (tons)	95	55	6	-
Coal and Coke handled	-	-	-	6
Trucks of livestock handled	-	-	-	-

Waterloo Tower

Wes. Meth. Chapel

Black Lion
(P.H.)

Mason's Arms
(P.H.)

Cefn Station

S.Ps

Ruabon..2
Chirk....3 3/4

M.S

Quarry
(Disused)

P.H.

Cefn-bychan

Quarry
(Disused)

P.H.

51.   The station opened in July 1849 and closed on 12th September 1960. The footbridge was added in 1913. An earlier station had been a quarter of a mile to the south. It was called Rhosymedre and was the terminus for two years. This view north is from 1950. (Stations UK)

52.   The staffing level varied: 7 in 1903, 5 in 1923 and 2 in 1933. No goods traffic was handled. We look south at the remains in 1965. (P.J.Garland/R.S.Carpenter)

RHOSYMEDRE HALT

53.   The halt was in use from 1st September 1906 to 2nd March 1959. This is a northward view from soon after its opening. (Stations UK)

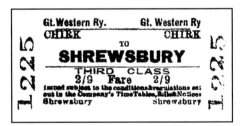

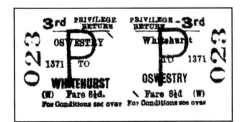

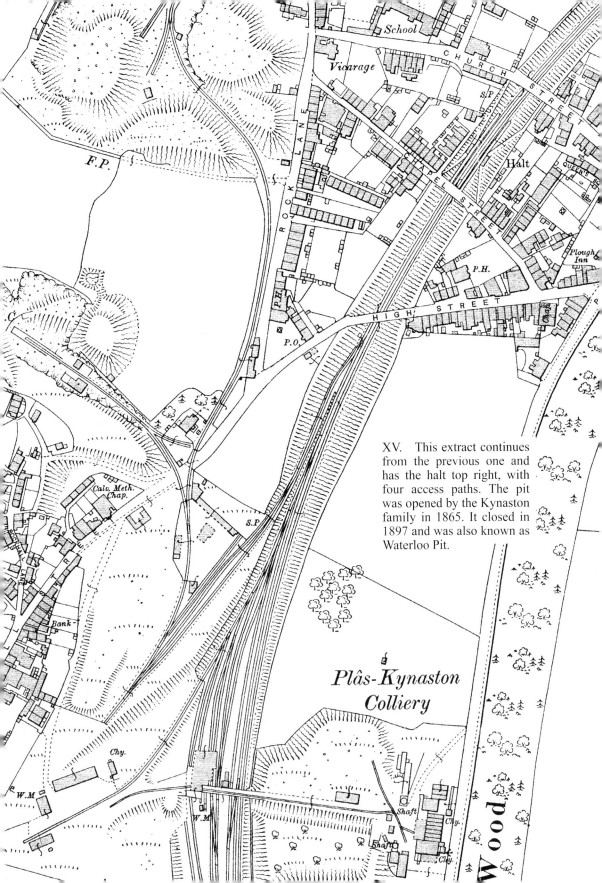

School

Vicarage

CHURCH STREET

S.P.

Halt

QUEEN'S

R
O
C
K

L
A
N
E

F.P.

Plough
Inn

P.H.

HIGH STREET

P.H.

Chap.

C

P.H.

P.O.

S.P.

XV. This extract continues
from the previous one and
has the halt top right, with
four access paths. The pit
was opened by the Kynaston
family in 1865. It closed in
1897 and was also known as
Waterloo Pit.

Calv. Meth.
Chap.

Bank

Plâs-Kynaston
Colliery

Chy.

W.M.

W.M.

Shaft

Chy.

Shaft

Clay.

W
o
o
d

SOUTH OF RUABON

54.   This is Llangollen Junction on 25th August 1962, as an express from Shrewsbury passes, hauled by 4-6-0 no.6823 *Brockton Grange*. It is seen from the signal box, which had 27 levers. (P.J.Garland/R.S.Carpenter)

55.   We are nearer to Ruabon and witness no. 7811 *Dunley Manor* southbound with a train destined for Barmouth. (P.J.Garland/R.S.Carpenter)

56.   Approaching Ru-
abon on 19th May 1951
is no. 3858, a 2-8-0 of the
2800 class. Wynnstay Col-
liery appears in this and the
previous view.
(H.Townley/Bentley coll.)

57.   Leaving   Ruabon
station on 18th April 1959
are nos 9018 and 9004,
4-4-0 "Dukedogs". They are
hauling the Festiniog Railway Society AGM special,
which had reversed in the
station. Your author (V.M.)
made the tiny headboard,
following criticism of the
large one of 1958, seen in
other albums. (G.Adams/
M.J.Stretton coll.)

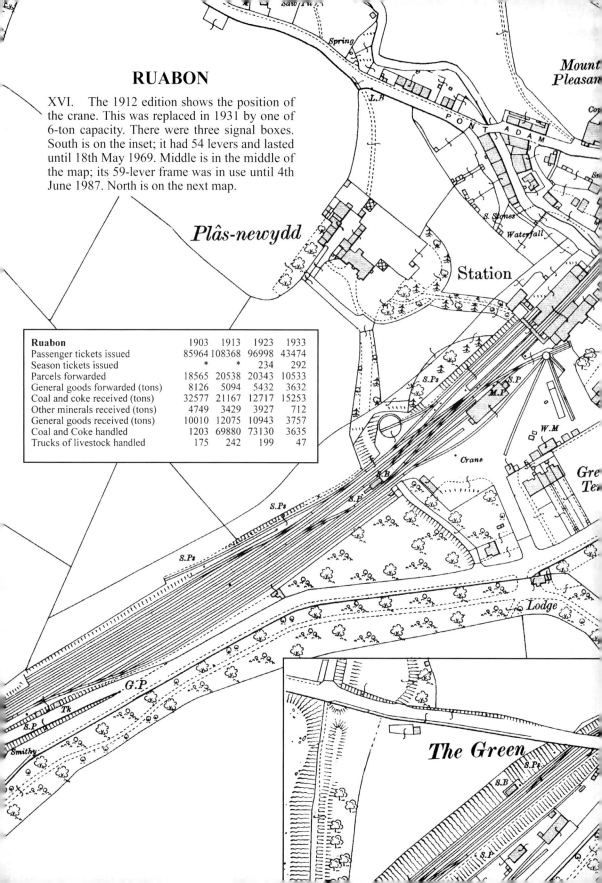

RUABON

XVI.   The 1912 edition shows the position of the crane. This was replaced in 1931 by one of 6-ton capacity. There were three signal boxes. South is on the inset; it had 54 levers and lasted until 18th May 1969. Middle is in the middle of the map; its 59-lever frame was in use until 4th June 1987. North is on the next map.

Plâs-newydd

Station

Mount Pleasant

Ruabon	1903	1913	1923	1933
Passenger tickets issued	85964	108368	96998	43474
Season tickets issued	*	*	234	292
Parcels forwarded	18565	20538	20343	10533
General goods forwarded (tons)	8126	5094	5432	3632
Coal and coke received (tons)	32577	21167	12717	15253
Other minerals received (tons)	4749	3429	3927	712
General goods received (tons)	10010	12075	10943	3757
Coal and Coke handled	1203	69880	73130	3635
Trucks of livestock handled	175	242	199	47

· Crane

Lodge

The Green

58.   The 3.56pm Ruabon to Bala Junction is ready to depart behind 0-6-0 no. 2259 on 12th
September 1952. The dock siding on the right differs from those shown on the map. (P.J.Kelley)

59.   A southward panorama from August 1960 has Middle Box in the middle and a curved track
to the turntable, right. The goods yard was in use until 7th December 1964.
(R.G.Nelson/T.Walsh)

60.   The footbridge had been widened in 1910 and a glazed canopy was provided in 1925. Present on 22nd April 1961 were no. 7824 *Iford Manor* and no. 7310, a 4300 class 2-6-0. (G.Adams/M.J.Stretton coll.)

61.   Staffing ceased on 4th February 1974 and a Shrewsbury-Chester DMU was recorded on 14th May 1977. The local population was around 3300 in the period 1900-1960. (C.L.Caddy)

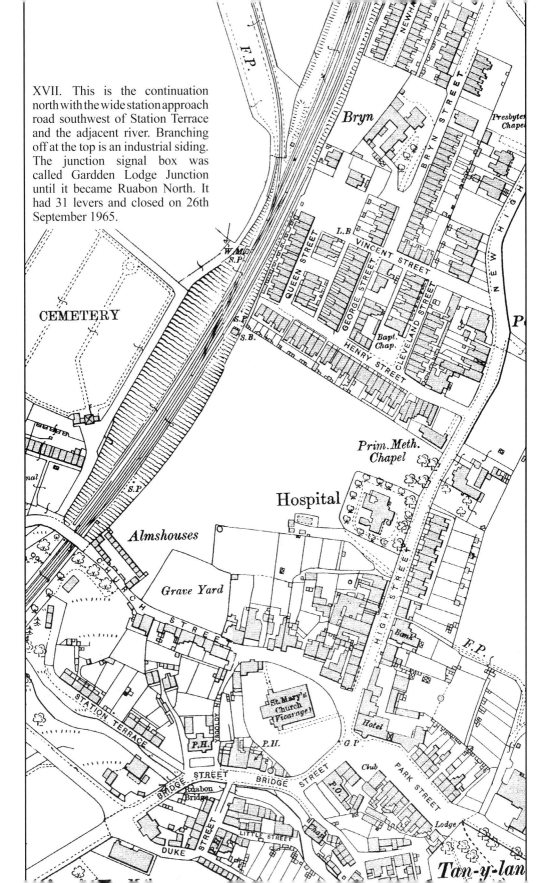

XVII. This is the continuation north with the wide station approach road southwest of Station Terrace and the adjacent river. Branching off at the top is an industrial siding. The junction signal box was called Gardden Lodge Junction until it became Ruabon North. It had 31 levers and closed on 26th September 1965.

F.P.

Bryn

NEW

Presbyter
Chapel

BRYN STREET

HIGH

W.M
S.P.

L.B

Queen Street

Vincent Street

George Street

Cleveland Street

CEMETERY

S.P.

S.B.

Bapt.
Chap.

HENRY STREET

P

S.P.

Prim. Meth.
Chapel

Hospital

Almshouses

CHURCH STREET

HIGH STREET

Grave Yard

Bank

F.P.

nal

STATION TERRACE

SAGDLY

St. Mary's
Church
Vicarage

Hotel

P.H.

P.H.

G.P.

Club

PARK STREET

STREET

BRIDGE STREET

P.O.

P.O.

Chap

BRIDGE STREET

Ruabon
Bridge

LITTLE STREET

DUKE

Lodge

Tan-y-lan

62.   A view in the other direction on the same day includes a bridge span to serve the house provided for the station master. The two structures soon vanished. Electric lighting had replaced gas in 1960. (C.L.Caddy)

63.   One of the then 'dedicated' fleet of Railfreight Metals locomotives based at Cardiff Canton, no. 37901 *Mirrlees Pioneer*, passes Ruabon with train 6Z42, the 11.30 'special' from Dee Marsh Junction to Margam, on 26th September 1987. The load is 22 empty BBA and BAA steel coil wagons. The signal box had been closed on 4th June 1987. It had 59 levers and had been termed "Middle" until 1969. (P.Shannon)

64. The scene on 27th June 2008 includes the well conserved building, which was in use as offices. Part of the footbridge is visible above the bus, which is one of many providing a speedy link to Llangollen. (V.Mitchell)

WYNNVILLE HALT

65. A southward view in 1961 reveals the urban surroundings. The halt was in use from 1st February 1934 until December 1960; oil lights were provided by the guards. The bridge on the right is shown near the bottom of map XVIII, on the next page. (Stations UK)

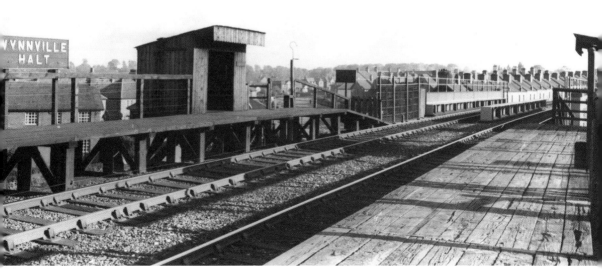

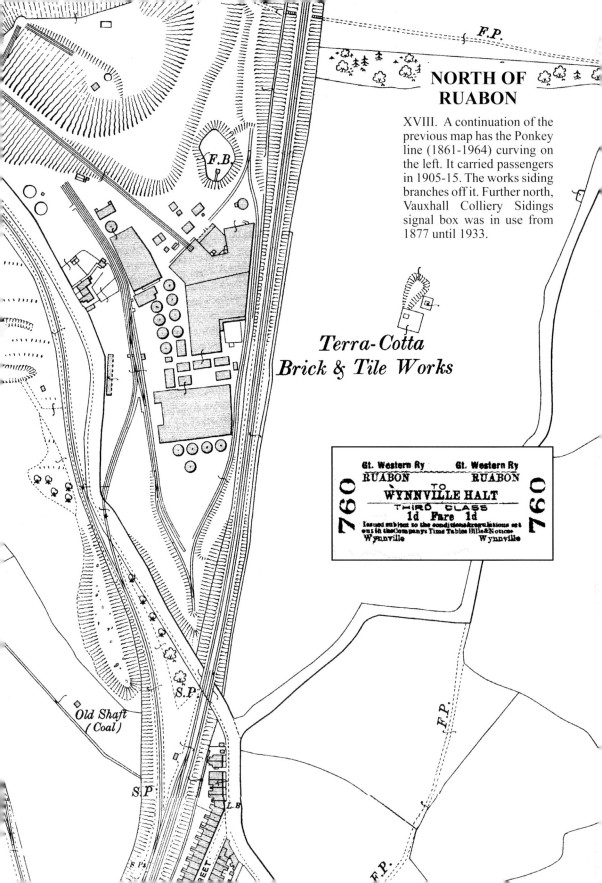

XVIII. A continuation of the previous map has the Ponkey line (1861-1964) curving on the left. It carried passengers in 1905-15. The works siding branches off it. Further north, Vauxhall Colliery Sidings signal box was in use from 1877 until 1933.

Terra-Cotta
Brick & Tile Works

F.B.

Gt. Western Ry   Gt. Western Ry
RUABON   **RUABON**
TO
WYNNVILLE HALT
THIRD CLASS
1d   Fare   1d
Issued subject to the conditions&regulations set out in the Company's Time Tables Bills&Notices
Wynnville   Wynnville

760   760

S.P.

Old Shaft
(Coal)

S.P.

L.B.

F.P.

F.P.

F.P.

JOHNSTOWN & HAFOD

XIX. The station opened on 1st June 1896 and is seen on the 1912 edition with Hafod brickworks and colliery sidings on the right. On the left is the 10-lever signal box, which served from 1880-1963. The colliery started in the 1860s as Ruabon New Colliery and eventually employed over 2000 men. Closure came on 11th March 1968.

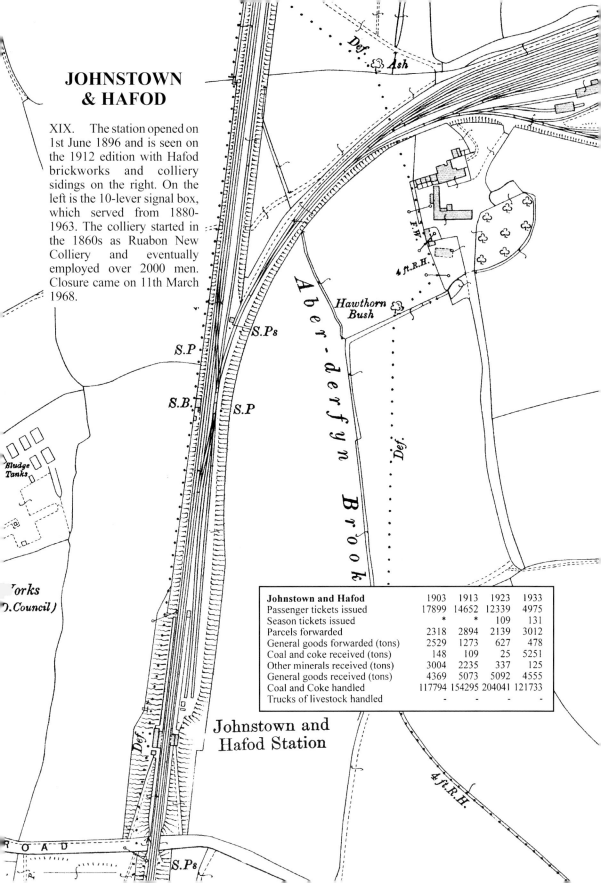

Johnstown and Hafod Station

Johnstown and Hafod	1903	1913	1923	1933
Passenger tickets issued	17899	14652	12339	4975
Season tickets issued	*	*	109	131
Parcels forwarded	2318	2894	2139	3012
General goods forwarded (tons)	2529	1273	627	478
Coal and coke received (tons)	148	109	25	5251
Other minerals received (tons)	3004	2235	337	125
General goods received (tons)	4369	5073	5092	4555
Coal and Coke handled	117794	154295	204041	121733
Trucks of livestock handled	-	-	-	-

66.   The station had a staff of eight in the 1930s and was photographed in 1961. North of it was Bersham signal box, which had a 19-lever frame in use from 1896 until 15th February 1987. (Stations UK)

67.   Staffing ceased on 1st June 1955 and closure came on 12th September 1960, after which time this photograph was taken looking north. Beyond Bersham was Rhos Junction Box (25 levers), it closing in 1955 although the branch carried freight until 1963. (Lens of Sutton coll.)

SOUTH OF
WREXHAM

XXa. The 1911 edition at 1ins to 1 mile shows the short-lived stations
and halts west of the main line at their optimum.

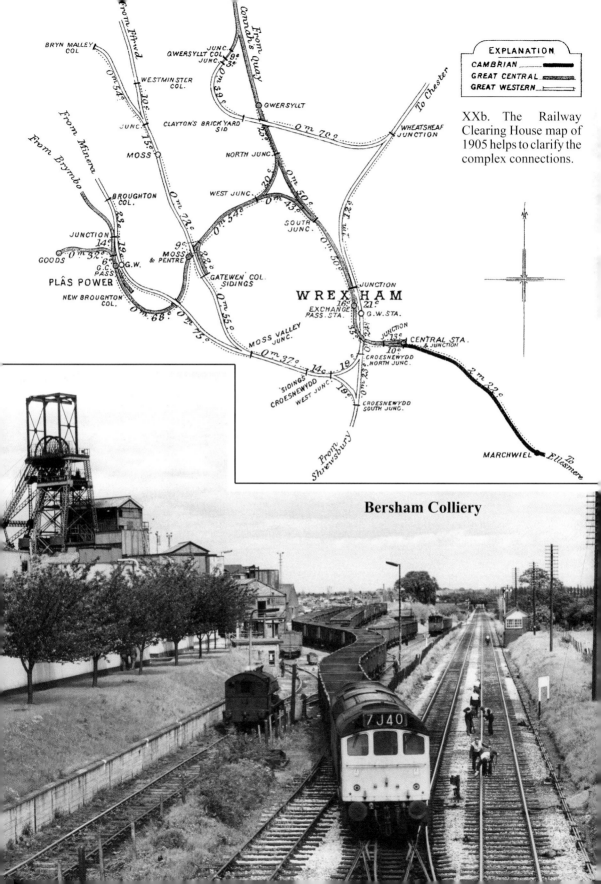

EXPLANATION
CAMBRIAN ——
GREAT CENTRAL ∙∙∙∙∙∙
GREAT WESTERN ——

XXb. The Railway Clearing House map of 1905 helps to clarify the complex connections.

BRYN MALLEY COL.

From Ffrwd

From Connah's Quay

JUNC.
GWERSYLLT COL. JUNC. 9c
3c

WESTMINSTER COL.

0 m 54c
10c

JUNC. 15c

CLAYTON'S BRICK YARD SID

GWERSYLLT

0 m 70c

To Chester

WHEATSHEAF JUNCTION

From Minera

MOSS

0 m 39c

NORTH JUNC.

From Brymbo

BROUGHTON COL.

0 m 72c

WEST JUNC.

23c 19c
JUNCTION 14c

0 m 32c

GOODS

G.W.

G.C. PASS.

PLÂS POWER

NEW BROUGHTON COL.

MOSS & PENTRE

0 m 54c

9c

22c

GATEWEN COL. SIDINGS

0 m 70c

0 m 50c

0 m 43c

SOUTH JUNC.

0 m 50c

7 m 72c

WREXHAM

16c 21c

EXCHANGE PASS. STA.

G.W. STA.

JUNCTION 13c

10c

CROESNEWYDD NORTH JUNC.

CENTRAL STA. & JUNCTION

2 m 29c

MARCHWIEL

To Ellesmere

0 m 68c

0 m 75c

0 m 55c

MOSS VALLEY JUNC.

0 m 37c

14c 19c

SIDINGS

CROESNEWYDD WEST JUNC.

19c

CROESNEWYDD SOUTH JUNC.

From Shrewsbury

Bersham Colliery

Croes Newydd South Junction

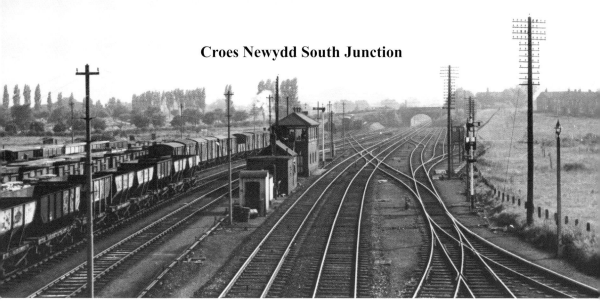

68. No. D5280 is propelling empty wagons into the sidings on 5th June 1972. On the left stands Hornet no. 1935 of 1937; it will undertake the shunting. The signal box is "Bersham Colliery" and it closed in December 1986. The colliery was sunk in 1867 and was closed in 1986. (T.Heavyside)

69. We look south from the road bridge below the engine shed on map XXI and find the branch on the right. The signal box was known as "South" or "South Fork" and its 60 levers were in use from 1909 until 5th February 1984. The photograph was taken in the Summer of 1965. (P.J.Garland/R.S.Carpenter)

70. A view from 12th July 1976 from the same location features no. 47049 with coke from the south. It will be shunted into the sidings on the right and later taken up the branch in short lengths to Brymbo Steelworks. (T.Heavyside)

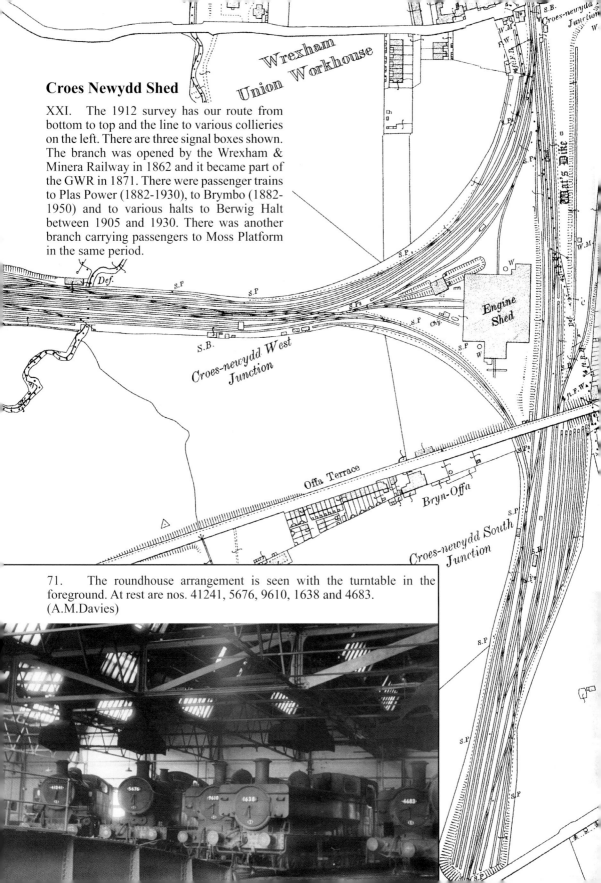

Croes Newydd Shed

XXI. The 1912 survey has our route from bottom to top and the line to various collieries on the left. There are three signal boxes shown. The branch was opened by the Wrexham & Minera Railway in 1862 and it became part of the GWR in 1871. There were passenger trains to Plas Power (1882-1930), to Brymbo (1882-1950) and to various halts to Berwig Halt between 1905 and 1930. There was another branch carrying passengers to Moss Platform in the same period.

Wrexham Union Workhouse

Def.

S.P

S.P

S.P

S.B.

Croes-newydd West Junction

Engine Shed

Offa Terrace

Bryn-Offa

Croes-newydd South Junction

Croes-newydd Junction

Wat's Dike

71. The roundhouse arrangement is seen with the turntable in the foreground. At rest are nos. 41241, 5676, 9610, 1638 and 4683. (A.M.Davies)

72.   The west elevation was recorded in 1966. The shed opened in 1902 and was coded CNYD. Under BR it was 84J until January 1961, when it became 89B. It was 6C from September 1963 until closure in March 1967. The shed was basically square with a central turntable. (S.K.Brown/D.K.Jones coll.)

73.   A standard GWR coal stage was provided, with the water tank providing the roof. It contained 45,000 gallons. An allocation of 39 locomotives was recorded on 31st December 1947. (A.M.Davies)

74.   The east elevation is seen in the Summer of 1965, along with part of Watery Lane Goods Depot. In the distance is North Fork signal box, which had 83 levers and now has a panel. (P.J.Garland/R.S.Carpenter)

Watery Road Sidings

75.   These two pictures were taken from the other side of the bridge used for pictures 69 and 70, the location being the top right corner of map XXI. No. 1660 is waiting to proceed south from the western siding. (B.W.L.Brooksbank)

Wrexham	1903	1913	1923	1933
Passenger tickets issued	314997	654365	464813	166331
Season tickets issued	*	*	917	1104
Parcels forwarded	81912	114525	122544	144495
General goods forwarded (tons)	15720	18784	8791	5204
Coal and coke received (tons)	19471	18988	16005	11162
Other minerals received (tons)	13229	8942	9216	8370
General goods received (tons)	24705	35969	29270	31695
Coal and Coke handled		212	160405	125182	278413
Trucks of livestock handled	585	483	509	333

↓ 76.   In the distance is Croes Newydd North Fork box, which was completed in 1940 with 83 levers. It was still in use in 2010 and controlled full barriers. No. 25055 is shunting on 12th July 1976, while a Type 2 stands on the left on the curve which once passed the engine shed. The goods yard closed for public traffic on 2nd March 1970. (T.Heavyside)

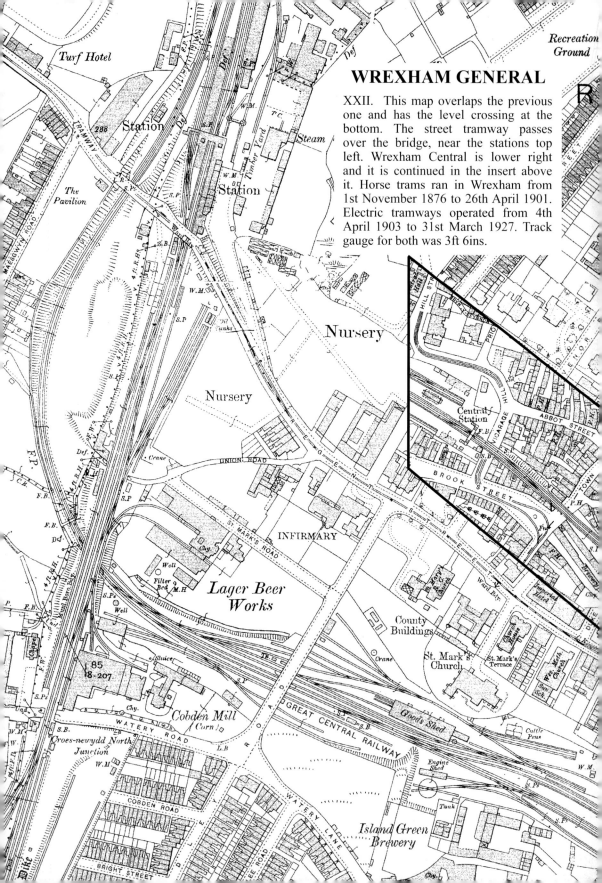

WREXHAM GENERAL

XXII. This map overlaps the previous one and has the level crossing at the bottom. The street tramway passes over the bridge, near the stations top left. Wrexham Central is lower right and it is continued in the insert above it. Horse trams ran in Wrexham from 1st November 1876 to 26th April 1901. Electric tramways operated from 4th April 1903 to 31st March 1927. Track gauge for both was 3ft 6ins.

Recreation Ground

R

Turf Hotel

Station

The Pavilion

Station

Steam

Tinker Yard

Nursery

Nursery

Central Station

HILL STREET

VICARAGE HILL

ABBOT STREET

BROOK STREET

UNION ROAD

INFIRMARY

ST MARK'S ROAD

Lager Beer Works

County Buildings

St. Mark's Church

St. Mark's Terrace

Cobden Mill

WATERY ROAD

Croes-nevydd North Junction

GREAT CENTRAL RAILWAY

Good's Shed

Engine Shed

Cattle Pens

Island Green Brewery

COBDEN ROAD

WATERY LANE

BRIGHT STREET

77.   This is the south end of the station in 1954 and on the left is South Box, which had a 69-lever frame in use from 1910 until 27th October 1968. One of the two bay platforms is on the right. (Stations UK)

78.   Moving to the other side of the road bridge, we can examine part of the island platform and 2-6-0 no. 6316 with a heavy load of coal. The station had been substantially rebuilt in 1910-12. (B.W.L.Brooksbank)

79.   The term "General" was added to the station on our route on 18th June 1951. We are on its island platform looking at the two Eastern Region platforms called "Exchange". They all had the suffix "General" from 1st June 1981, but only one of the latter two was in use.
(Lens of Sutton coll.)

80.   A southward panorama from the road bridge on 21st June 1959 includes part of the long up platform, one of the bays, the cattle dock and the hospital. The staff totalled 114 in 1923 and 104 in 1938. (P.J.Garland/R.S.Carpenter)

81.   Looking north along the main down platform in August 1960, we have our first glimpse of the massive goods shed, which was still standing 50 years later. The town had a population of 36,120 recorded in 1961. (R.G.Nelson/T.Wright)

82.   Most of the up platform was photographed on 10th August 1960, along with South Box. The station had received electric lights in about 1955, but the engine shed had them from 1930. (R.G.Nelson/T.Wright)

83.　　A 1964 view gives an impression of the extent of the goods offices and includes 0-6-2T no. 6694, one of the 5600 class introduced in 1924 for service in the South Wales valleys. (A.M.Davies)

84.　　Standing at the south end of the station on 27th August 1964 is sister engine no. 6651. Goods traffic was substantial and a 12-ton crane was listed in 1938. (H.C.Casserley)

85.	A Shrewsbury to Chester DMU is arriving on 18th September 1980, as a parcels train takes a rest. The line to Wrexham Central passes under the main line near the white wall in the distance. The plates on the right once aided cattle wagon cleaning. (T.Heavyside)

86.	We finish our survey with three photographs from 26th June 2008. A train bound for Cardiff Central is on the right, while a W&SR train stands at platform 3, waiting to return to Marylebone. The firm became part of Chiltern Railways in December 2009. (V.Mitchell)

87.　　The four coaches of the same train are in the background as we examine the remnants of Wrexham Exchange and the associated vegetation. It is possible to travel to Wrexham Central from here, but it is 400yds short of the original station of that name. (V.Mitchell)

88.　　GWR detailing could still be enjoyed on the east elevation and a staffed ticket office gave a traditional ambiance. The provision of direct trains to London and Holyhead was an unexpected and welcome recent development. (V.Mitchell)

NORTH OF WREXHAM

89.   The platform starting signals are on the right in this northward view from 21st June 1959. The ringed signals are for freight. The 1883 North Box is evident; it had 36 levers. (P.J.Garland/R.S.Carpenter)

90.   A short train from Chester is about to terminate on 5th June 1982. The rear coach is in line with North Box, which closed on 16th March 1986. The signals had all changed. The class 25 on the left is on the former Great Central route. The connection in the middle is to the line to Bidston, which receives a regular service from Wrexham Central. (T.Heavyside)

RHOSROBIN HALT

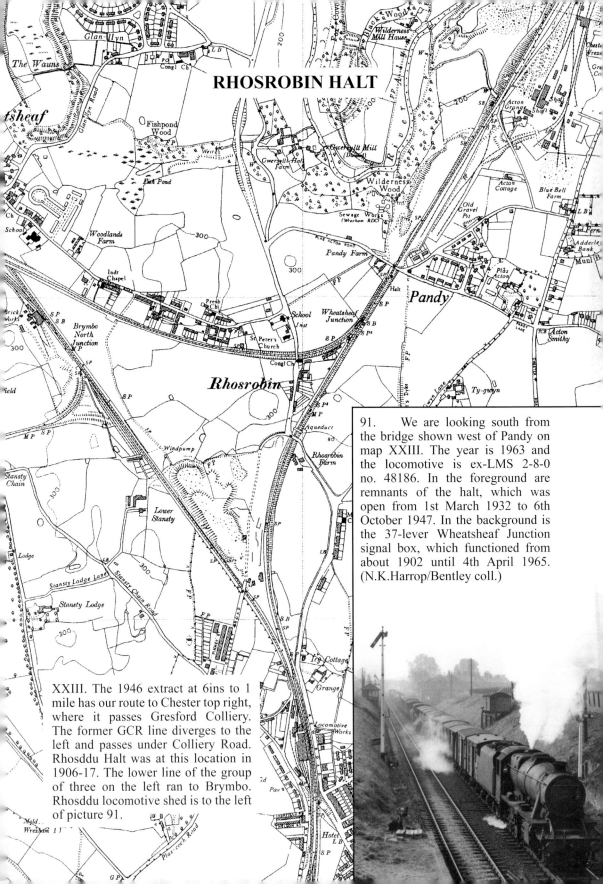

91.   We are looking south from the bridge shown west of Pandy on map XXIII. The year is 1963 and the locomotive is ex-LMS 2-8-0 no. 48186. In the foreground are remnants of the halt, which was open from 1st March 1932 to 6th October 1947. In the background is the 37-lever Wheatsheaf Junction signal box, which functioned from about 1902 until 4th April 1965. (N.K.Harrop/Bentley coll.)

XXIII. The 1946 extract at 6ins to 1 mile has our route to Chester top right, where it passes Gresford Colliery. The former GCR line diverges to the left and passes under Colliery Road. Rhosddu Halt was at this location in 1906-17. The lower line of the group of three on the left ran to Brymbo. Rhosddu locomotive shed is to the left of picture 91.

SOUTH OF GRESFORD

92.　　The first two views of Gresford Colliery are from the Summer of 1965. Here we look north at the inevitable waste tips and note that the running lines drop steeply relative to the level sidings. (P.J.Garland/R.S.Carpenter)

93.　　The pit was productive from June 1911, working three seams at over 90°F. We now have the view south, with the main lines on the right. The 41-lever signal box was called "United Colliery" and was destroyed by fire in June 1970. Its replacement was in use from 9th August 1970 until 1st October 1974; parts of it later went to the Llangollen Railway. (N.K.Harrop/Bentley coll.)

94.   Closure of the colliery came in 1973. No. D5038 was leaving the exchange sidings when photographed on 5th June 1972. The pit suffered a massive disaster on 22nd September 1934, when 265 men lost their lives. (T.Heavyside)

95.   No. 35028 *Clan Line* is passing the derelict colliery on 26th April 1975 with a Chester to Hereford special. It has a climb of 1 in 82 for around three miles. (T.Heavyside)

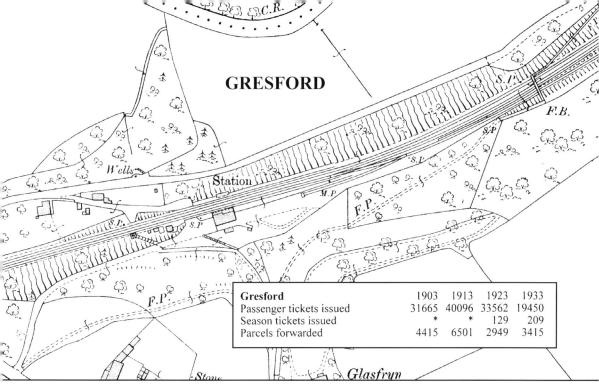

GRESFORD

Gresford	1903	1913	1923	1933
Passenger tickets issued	31665	40096	33562	19450
Season tickets issued	*	*	129	209
Parcels forwarded	4415	6501	2949	3415

XXIV. The 1912 survey includes a public footbridge with steps on one side only, as it was on the valley side. The village housed 1108 in 1901, rising to 2063 in 1961. The suffix "for Llay" was added in about 1923.

96. A postcard reveals the early low platform level and the elegant small canopy. The signal box was built in 1883 and was fitted with a new 13-lever frame in 1911. It closed on 30th December 1956 and the station was downgraded to a halt in 1960. (Lens of Sutton coll.)

97.   Another early postcard and this gives more architectural detail, plus a glimpse of the down shelter in decline. There were four men employed here in the 1930s. Staffing ceased on 2nd May 1955. (D.Giddins coll.)

98.   The station was about halfway up the severe climb and a refuge or holding siding was provided. A "Hall" class 4-6-0 is creeping down the 1 in 82 gradient. Passenger trains ceased to call on 10th September 1962. The headcode was for "Express freight", which meant 35mph maximum and a minimum of five vacuum braked vehicles next to the engine. (D.Giddins coll.)

99.   Struggling hard on "Gresford Bank" on 3rd June 1961 is no. 4990 *Clifton Hall*. The canopy and the level crossing had gone, but the replacement down shelter remained, as did the 9.0am from Bala and the 6.12pm to Barmouth, on weekdays. These were the only trains to call after September 1960. This goods train was allowed 45mph, as it had remotely operated brakes on at least one third of the wagons. (D.Giddins coll.)

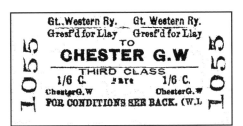

Gt. Western Ry.   Gt. Western Ry.
Gresf'd for Llay   Gresf'd for Llay
TO
CHESTER G.W
THIRD CLASS
1/6 C.   Fare   1/6 C.
ChesterG.W   ChesterG.W
FOR CONDITIONS SEE BACK. (W.L

1055   1055

Gt. Western Ry.   Gt. Western Ry
GRESFORD   GRESFORD
for LLAY   for LLAY
TO
WREXHAM
THIRD   CLASS
5d Fare 5d
Issued subject to the conditions & regulations set out in the Company's Time Tables, Bills & Notices
Wrexham   Wrexham

2617   2617

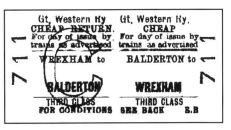

Gt. Western Ry.   Gt. Western Ry.
CHEAP RETURN   CHEAP
For day of issue by   For day of issue by
trains as advertised   trains as advertised
WREXHAM to   BALDERTON to
BALDERTON   WREXHAM
THIRD CLASS   THIRD CLASS
FOR CONDITIONS SEE BACK   E.B

711   711

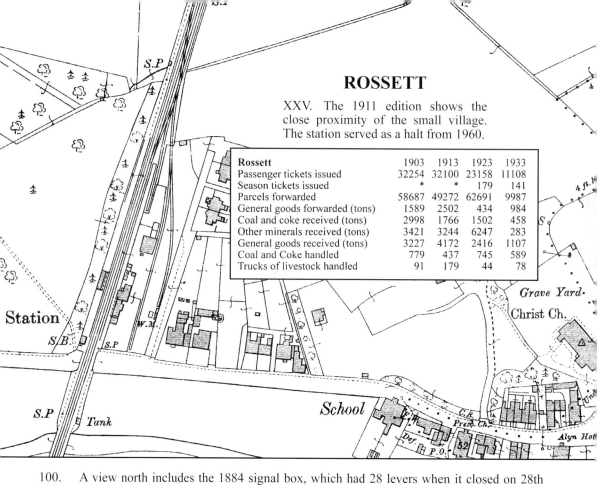

ROSSETT

XXV. The 1911 edition shows the close proximity of the small village. The station served as a halt from 1960.

Rossett	1903	1913	1923	1933
Passenger tickets issued	32254	32100	23158	11108
Season tickets issued	*	*	179	141
Parcels forwarded	58687	49272	62691	9987
General goods forwarded (tons)	1589	2502	434	984
Coal and coke received (tons)	2998	1766	1502	458
Other minerals received (tons)	3421	3244	6247	283
General goods received (tons)	3227	4172	2416	1107
Coal and Coke handled	779	437	745	589
Trucks of livestock handled	91	179	44	78

100.   A view north includes the 1884 signal box, which had 28 levers when it closed on 28th February 1960. It was replaced by another box, which lasted until the singling on 2nd February 1986. (Lens of Sutton coll.)

101.   The station opened after its neighbours, on 4th November 1866, and closed after them, on 26th October 1964. The goods yard was in use until 6th October 1968. There was a staff of 14 to 16 in the 1930s. We look northwards in 1959. After closure, trains continued to call for the pupils of Moreton Hall School. (P.J.Garland/R.S.Carpenter)

102.   No. 25268 passes with train 6F81, the 15.21 Dee Marsh Junction to Warrington Arpley Speedlink trip working, on 19th April 1985. The train is carrying two empty BBAs from Shotton, five POAs with scrap from Shotton to Sheffield, and one PCA with cement from Penyffordd. (P.Shannon)

BALDERTON

Balderton Station

Balderton Bridge

S.P

S.B

W.M.

Stone

S.P

C.

Cattle
Pens

W.M.

S.P

XXVI.   The 1911 map includes the 53yd long Balderton Tunnel and the private siding for Eaton Hall, which was three miles to the east. There had been a station two miles south of here at Pulford until about 1858 but its siding was open to public traffic until 18th July 1959.

The 15ins gauge Eaton Railway of the Duke of Westminster supplied the Hall, but did not carry the public. It opened in 1896 and is seen in about 1900. It closed in 1946 and most items went to the Romney Hythe & Dymchurch Railway, which is still running. The 0-4-0T *Katie* is shunting. There were also two 0-6-0Ts, *Shelagh* and *Ursula*, plus two petrol locomotives. Journey time was 20 minutes. (A.Dudman coll.)

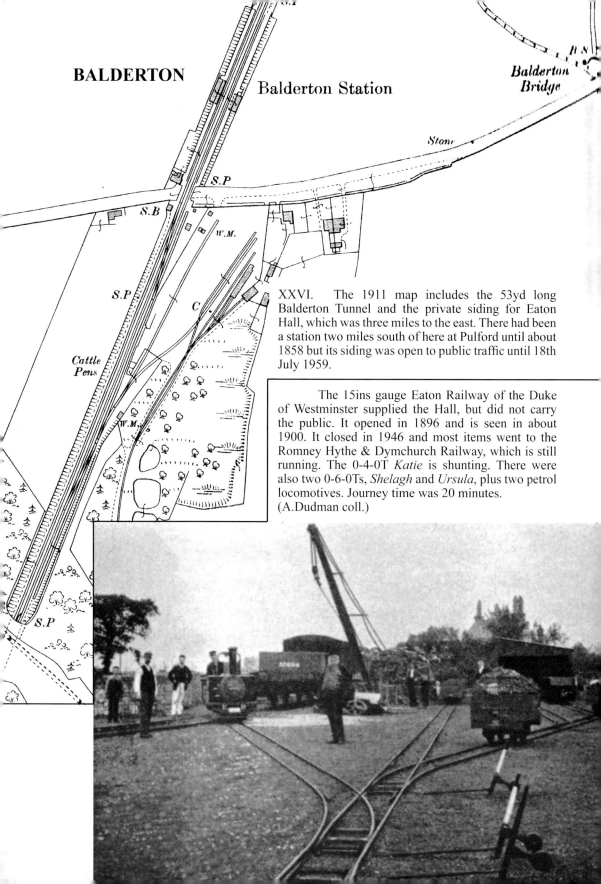

103. GWR architecture is evident as the station did not open until 1st July 1901, although the sidings probably came into use earlier. This view north is from 1954; the station had closed on 3rd March 1952. (Stations UK)

Balderton	1903	1913	1923	1933
Passenger tickets issued	6367	5904	4974	1794
Season tickets issued	*	*	37	2
Parcels forwarded	13420	12090	14556	9649
General goods forwarded (tons)	109	238	108	30
Coal and coke received (tons)	3315	3269	2334	478
Other minerals received (tons)	2410	1862	1095	1056
General goods received (tons)	1109	827	418	134
Coal and Coke handled	202	165	37	1213
Trucks of livestock handled	25	40	63	23

104. Another red lamp glass is included in this 1965 picture. The box of 1898 had 23 levers when it closed on 17th October 1965. The local goods traffic ceased on 1st November 1954. To the north was Green Lane Crossing; its 21-lever frame was in use until 4th January 1986. The box was moved to the Llangollen Railway. (P.J.Garland/R.S.Carpenter)

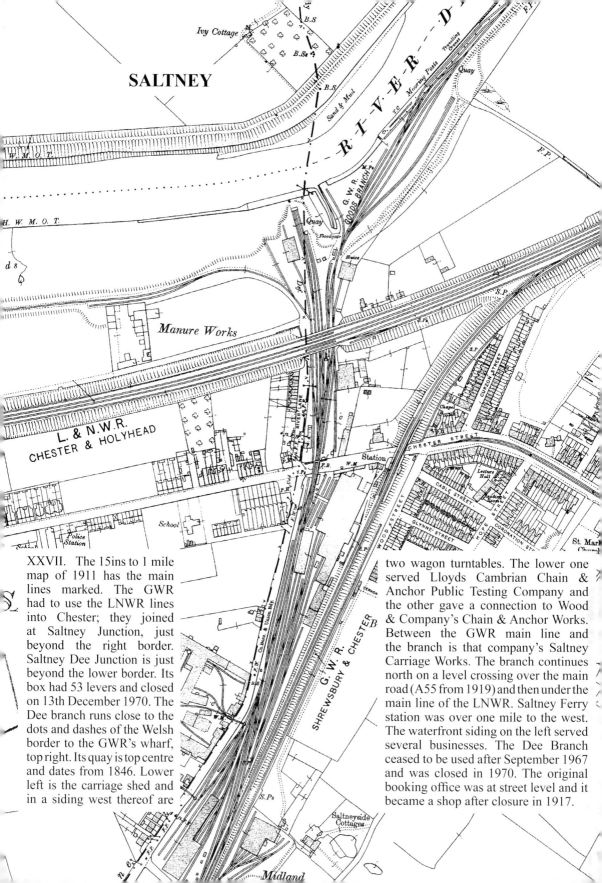

SALTNEY

Ivy Cottage

RIVER D

Quay

Manure Works

L. & N.W.R.
CHESTER & HOLYHEAD

G.W.R. GOODS BRANCH

Station

CURZON STREET

CHESTER STREET

CABLE STREET

GLYNNE STREET

CORONATION STREET

Lecture Hall

School

Police Station

WOOD STREET

G.W.R. SHREWSBURY & CHESTER

Saltneyside Cottages

Midland

XXVII. The 15ins to 1 mile map of 1911 has the main lines marked. The GWR had to use the LNWR lines into Chester; they joined at Saltney Junction, just beyond the right border. Saltney Dee Junction is just beyond the lower border. Its box had 53 levers and closed on 13th December 1970. The Dee branch runs close to the dots and dashes of the Welsh border to the GWR's wharf, top right. Its quay is top centre and dates from 1846. Lower left is the carriage shed and in a siding west thereof are two wagon turntables. The lower one served Lloyds Cambrian Chain & Anchor Public Testing Company and the other gave a connection to Wood & Company's Chain & Anchor Works. Between the GWR main line and the branch is that company's Saltney Carriage Works. The branch continues north on a level crossing over the main road (A55 from 1919) and then under the main line of the LNWR. Saltney Ferry station was over one mile to the west. The waterfront siding on the left served several businesses. The Dee Branch ceased to be used after September 1967 and was closed in 1970. The original booking office was at street level and it became a shop after closure in 1917.

105. The tram terminus is shown on the map, east of the station. The tramway was 3ft 6ins gauge and operated electrically from 6th April 1904. A horse-drawn system had started with standard gauge track in 1879. Closure came on 15th February 1930. The *Chester Tramways* album (Middleton Press) will take you on a journey through the streets of the city to Chester General. (A.Dudman coll.)

106. An aerial view features Saltney Carriage Works a few years after it had closed in 1932. We are looking south, with the station on the left. The A55 runs across the foreground and parallel to it is a footbridge provided to minimise delays to local people during the prolonged shunting operations on the branch. The up marshalling yard is in the background. The building with the white roof had originally been the locomotive works of the S&CR. Lower left is the wagon sheet repair works. (A.Dudman coll.)

107.   A northward view in 1951 shows the station, which opened on 4th July 1932. The first one opened with the line and was a little further north, on the road bridge. It closed on 1st January 1917 as a wartime economy measure, having been used for ticket inspection for many years. Final closure came on 12th September 1960, but the goods yard lasted until May 1967. (Stations UK)

XXVIII.   The Railway Clearing House map of 1903 has our route lower left. Marshalling yards were developed: on the down side were two loops and 12 sidings, while on the up side were two loops with 17 sidings.

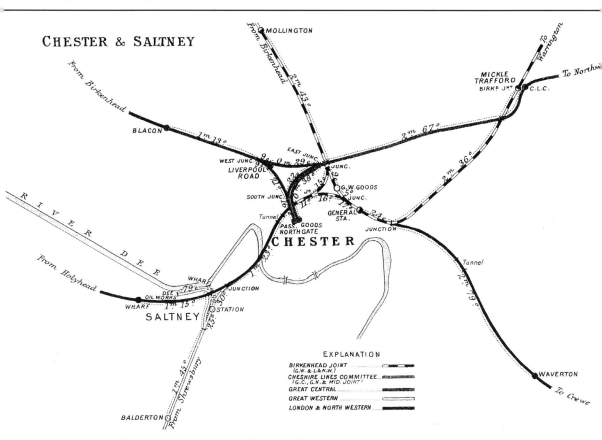

108.   The wharf was equipped with an early travelling crane (right) and a later one (left). Goods inward included iron ore from Cumberland and Spain for Brymbo Ironworks, plus slates and timber for local use. Outward was coal and limestone, notably. In 1872, 884 ships moved 107,670 tons of merchandise. (Postcard)

109.   Saltney Junction is seen from the signal box of that name in the 1960s, with Chester in the background. The LNWR quadrupled its main line in this vicinity in June 1903 and the trackwork was then much as seen, although the line on the right was a loop, not a siding. The box had 60 levers and was in use until 25th February 1973. The up (fast) pair of tracks were removed in October 1979, simplifying the junction and 1986 brought the singling to Wrexham. (A.Dudman coll.)

SOUTH OF CHESTER

110. Chester is on the skyline as no. 47335 passes over the River Dee with a Freightliner container train for Holyhead on 30th June 1988. Chester Racecourse is on the right and the old spans are on the left. The first bridge was designed by Robert Stephenson and comprised cast iron girders on two stone piers. One section collapsed when the 6.15pm to Ruabon was passing over it on 24th May 1847. There were four deaths. The bridge was rebuilt with wrought iron in 1871. (T.Heavyside)

111.   Leaving Chester on 5th June 1982 is the 19.20 to Shrewsbury. It is passing under No. 6 Box (80 levers), which was in use from July 1903 until 5th May 1984. The DMU will soon pass the site of Crane Street Box (15 levers), which closed on 16th April 1967. On the left is the curve which allowed trains between Birkenhead and the South of England to avoid reversing at Chester. The house on the right is at the north end of Cornwall Street, shown on the next map. (T.Heavyside)

CHESTER

112.   This atmospheric photograph seems worthy of inclusion, although no information is available about it. Apart from some extra platforms in 1905, the station has changed little, much of the original brickwork still being in place, but not all the roofing exists. (Lens of Sutton coll.)

113.   The suffix "General" was used inconsistently and was officially dropped on 6th May 1970.   Ex-Caledonian Railway 4-2-2 no. 123 is standing with an exhibition train on 10th August 1953. (H.C.Casserley)

114.   The impressive south facade was recorded on 23rd March 1958. Little had changed 50 years later and some tram track could still be found in nearby side streets. The terminus had been in the foreground - see map. (R.M.Casserley)

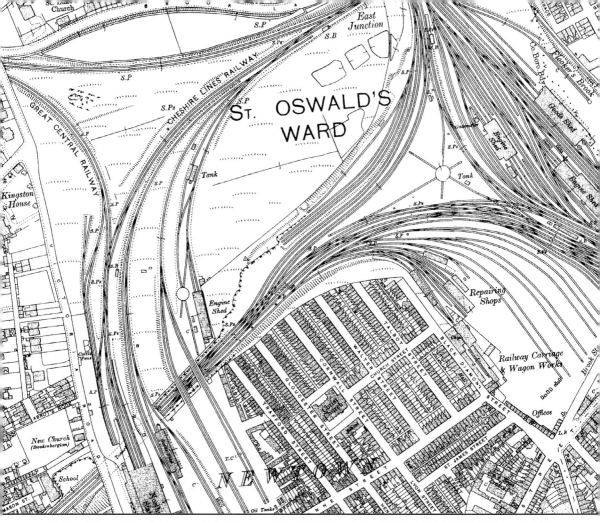

115.   The engine shed was originally that of the C&BR and the GWR coded it CHR. BR used 84K and then 6E from February 1958. A new shed was built in brick in the mid-1950s, but closure came in April 1960. The locomotive allocation was 51 in 1947. Centre stage is ex-LMS 4-6-0 no. 45015 on 10th July 1954. The four signal boxes west of the station all closed in May 1984. (B.W.L.Brooksbank)

XXIX. The 1911 edition is at 15ins to 1 mile. The GWR goods shed is on the right of the left page; goods staff numbered around 40 in the 1930s, but the passenger station was manned jointly with the LMS. Its engine shed is near the turntable, while the GWR one is below its goods shed. The route from Saltney is lower left; it passes through Northgate Street Tunnel (218yds) and then Windmill Lane Tunnel (104yds). Quadruple track was still in place in this vicinity in 2010. The Birkenhead lines converge at the top. Northgate station (lower left) closed on 6th October 1969; its goods yard shut on 5th April 1965. The General Yard handled coal until November 1970. Chester's main gasworks was to the left of picture 110. No siding was provided because of construction difficulties, so up to 64,000 tons of coal per annum (the 1950 total) were unloaded at Northgate yard and carted to the gasworks. There were two railway-owned plants for making carriage gas at Chester General, the GWR plant being beside their locomotive shed, while the LNWR equivalent was within the station area. Chester United Gas Company provided the station's needs from 1905.

116.   No. 73033 was a BR class 5 4-6-0 of the type introduced in 1951 and is seen on 19th September 1959. The roof remnants gave the station a shabby appearance for many years. (H.C.Casserley)

117.   "Patriot" class 4-6-0 no. 45534 *E.Tootal Broadhurst* is prominent, with two "Black Fives", three 2-6-4Ts and 2-6-0 no. 78033 in attendance. This is the view west on 4th August 1962, after some of the roof structure had been removed. (B.W.L.Brooksbank)

118.   Platform 3 (left) can accommodate 18 coaches, no. 4 takes 15, both no. 5 and no. 6 take 5 and the electrified no. 7 has room for 15. On the right in green livery is a Llandudno to Crewe DMU, while nearest on the left is a "Sprinter" bound for Wrexham on 30th June 1988. (T.Heavyside)

119.   Maintenance sheds were built on the site of the engine sheds and are seen from the west end of platform 3 on 7th September 2009. The white boards on the track mark the position of conductor rails laid in 1992 to provide an electric service north to Hooton and Liverpool. The line on the left is to the west bay platform numbered 2. (V.Mitchell)

Chester	1903	1913	1923	1933
Passenger tickets issued	106608	103957	111071	61321
Season tickets issued	*	*	398	567
Parcels forwarded	48909	69983	63951	75469
General goods forwarded (tons)	15567	14205	6641	4500
Coal and coke received (tons)	18607	27130	36456	25098
Other minerals received (tons)	8278	7547	8927	3576
General goods received (tons)	9880	11769	7218	7672
Coal and Coke handled	5010	26696	4408	4531
Trucks of livestock handled	635	505	594	426

120.   Seen on the same day is the 10.10 Super Voyager from Euston, having terminated at platform 1. It is no. 221114. The former parcels platform on the left was not numbered. It was the first year for Chester to have a train direct from London almost every hour. Three continued to Holyhead and the 18.10 divided to provide a portion for Wrexham General, arrival being due at 20.46. The best service ever for Chester! (V.Mitchell)

MP Middleton Press
EVOLVING THE ULTIMATE RAIL ENCYCLOPEDIA

Easebourne Lane, Midhurst, West Sussex.
GU29 9AZ   Tel:01730 813169

www.middletonpress.co.uk   email:info@middletonpress.co.uk
A-978 0 906520 B- 978 1 873793 C- 978 1 901706 D-978 1 904474 E- 978 1 906008

All titles listed below were in print at time of publication - please check current availability by looking at our website - **www.middletonpress.co.uk** or by requesting a Brochure which includes our *LATEST* RAILWAY TITLES also our TRAMWAY, TROLLEYBUS, MILITARY and WATERWAYS series

A
Abergavenny to Merthyr C 91 8
Abertillery and Ebbw Vale Lines D 84 5
Allhallows - Branch Line to A 62 8
Alton - Branch Lines to A 11 6
Andover to Southampton A 82 6
Ascot - Branch Lines around A 64 2
Ashburton - Branch Line to A 76 8
Ashford - Steam to Eurostar B 67 1
Ashford to Dover A 48 2
Austrian Narrow Gauge D 04 3
Avonmouth - BL around D 42 5
Aylesbury to Rugby D 91 3

B
Baker Street to Uxbridge D 90 6
Banbury to Birmingham D 27 2
Banbury to Cheltenham E 63 5
Barking to Southend C 80 2
Barmouth to Pwllheli E 53 6
Barry - Branch Lines around D 50 0
Bath Green Park to Bristol C 36 9
Bath to Evercreech Junction A 60 4
Bedford to Wellingborough D 31 9
Birmingham to Wolverhampton E 25 3
Bletchley to Cambridge D 94 4
Bletchley to Rugby E 07 9
Bodmin - Branch Lines around B 83 1
Bournemouth & Poole Trys B 47 3
Bournemouth to Evercreech Jn A 46 8
Bournemouth to Weymouth A 57 4
Brecon to Neath D 43 2
Brecon to Newport D 16 6
Brecon to Newtown E 06 2
Brighton to Eastbourne A 16 1
Brighton to Worthing A 03 1
Bromley South to Rochester B 23 7
Bromsgrove to Birmingham D 87 6
Bromsgrove to Gloucester D 73 9
Brunel - A railtour of his achievements D 74 6
Bude - Branch Line to B 29 9
Burnham to Evercreech Junction B 68 0

C
Cambridge to Ely D 55 5
Canterbury - Branch Lines around B 58 9
Cardiff to Dowlais (Cae Harris) E 47 5
Cardiff to Swansea E 42 0
Carmarthen to Fishguard E 66 6
Caterham & Tattenham Corner B 25 1
Chard and Yeovil - BLs around C 30 7
Charing Cross to Dartford A 75 8
Charing Cross to Orpington A 96 3
Cheddar - Branch Line to B 90 9
Cheltenham to Andover C 43 7
Cheltenham to Redditch D 81 4
Chichester to Portsmouth A 14 7
Clapham Junction to Beckenham Jn B 36 7
Cleobury Mortimer - BLs around E 18 5
Clevedon & Portishead - BLs to D 18 0
Colonel Stephens D 62 3
Consett to South Shields E 57 4
Cornwall Narrow Gauge D 56 2
Corris and Vale of Rheidol E 65 9
Craven Arms to Llandeilo E 35 2
Craven Arms to Wellington E 33 8
Crawley to Littlehampton A 34 5
Cromer - Branch Lines around C 26 0
Croydon to East Grinstead B 48 0
Crystal Palace and Catford Loop B 87 1
Cyprus Narrow Gauge E 13 0

D
Darlington - Leamside - Newcastle E 28 4
Darlington to Newcastle D 98 2
Dartford to Sittingbourne B 34 3
Derwent Valley - Branch Line to the D 06 7
Devon Narrow Gauge E 09 3
Didcot to Banbury D 02 9
Didcot to Swindon C 84 0
Didcot to Winchester C 13 0
Dorset & Somerset Narrow Gauge D 76 0

Douglas to Peel C 88 8
Douglas to Port Erin C 55 0
Douglas to Ramsey D 39 5
Dover to Ramsgate A 78 9
Dublin Northwards in the 1950s E 31 4
Dunstable - Branch Lines to E 27 7

E
Ealing to Slough C 42 0
East Cornwall Mineral Railways D 22 7
East Croydon to Three Bridges A 53 6
Eastern Spain Narrow Gauge E 56 7
East Grinstead - Branch Lines to A 07 9
East London - Branch Lines of C 44 4
East London Line B 80 0
East of Norwich - Branch Lines E 69 7
Effingham Junction - BLs around A 74 1
Ely to Norwich C 90 1
Enfield Town & Palace Gates - BL to D 32 6
Epsom to Horsham A 30 7
Eritrean Narrow Gauge E 38 3
Euston to Harrow & Wealdstone C 89 5
Exeter to Barnstaple B 15 2
Exeter to Newton Abbot C 49 9
Exeter to Tavistock B 69 5
Exmouth - Branch Lines to B 00 8

F
Fairford - Branch Line to A 52 9
Falmouth, Helston & St. Ives - BL to C 74 1
Fareham to Salisbury A 67 3
Faversham to Dover B 05 3
Felixstowe & Aldeburgh - BL to D 20 3
Fenchurch Street to Barking C 20 8
Festiniog - 50 yrs of enterprise C 83 3
Festiniog 1946-55 E 01 7
Festiniog in the Fifties B 68 8
Festiniog in the Sixties B 91 6
Finsbury Park to Alexandra Palace C 02 8
Frome to Bristol B 77 0

G
Gloucester to Bristol D 35 7
Gloucester to Cardiff D 66 1
Gosport - Branch Lines around A 36 9
Greece Narrow Gauge D 72 2

H
Hampshire Narrow Gauge D 36 4
Harrow to Watford D 14 2
Hastings to Ashford A 37 6
Hawkhurst - Branch Line to A 66 6
Hayling - Branch Line to A 12 3
Hay-on-Wye - Branch Lines around D 92 0
Haywards Heath to Seaford A 39 8
Hemel Hempstead - Branch Lines to D 88 3
Henley, Windsor & Marlow - BL to C77 2
Hereford to Newport D 54 8
Hertford and Hatfield - BLs around E 58 1 6
Hexham to Carlisle D 75 3
Hitchin to Peterborough D 07 4
Holborn Viaduct to Lewisham A 81 9
Horsham - Branch Lines to A 02 4
Huntingdon - Branch Line to A 93 2

I
Ilford to Shenfield C 97 0
Ilfracombe - Branch Line to B 21 3
Industrial Rlys of the South East A 09 3
Ipswich to Saxmundham C 41 3
Isle of Wight Lines - 50 yrs C 12 3

K
Kent Narrow Gauge C 45 1
Kidderminster to Shrewsbury E 10 9
Kingsbridge - Branch Line to C 98 7
Kings Cross to Potters Bar E 62 8
Kingston & Hounslow Loops A 83 3
Kingswear - Branch Line to C 17 8

L
Lambourn - Branch Line to C 70 3
Launceston & Princetown - BL to C 19 2
Lewisham to Dartford A 92 5
Lines around Wimbledon B 75 6

Liverpool Street to Chingford D 01 2
Liverpool Street to Ilford C 34 5
Llandeilo to Swansea E 46 8
London Bridge to Addiscombe B 20 6
London Bridge to East Croydon A 58 1
Longmoor - Branch Lines to A 41 3
Looe - Branch Line to C 22 2
Lowestoft - Branch Lines around E 40 6
Ludlow to Hereford E 14 7
Lydney - Branch Lines around E 26 0
Lyme Regis - Branch Line to A 45 1
Lynton - Branch Line to B 04 6

M
Machynlleth to Barmouth E 54 3
March - Branch lines around B 09 1
Marylebone to Rickmansworth D 49 4
Melton Constable to Yarmouth Beach E 03 1
Mexborough to Swinton E 36 9
Midhurst - Branch Lines around A 49 9
Mitcham Junction Lines B 01 5
Mitchell & company C 59 8
Monmouth - Branch Lines to E 20 8
Monmouthshire Eastern Valleys D 71 5
Moretonhampstead - BL to C 27 7
Moreton-in-Marsh to Worcester D 26 5
Mountain Ash to Neath D 80 7

N
Newbury to Westbury C 66 6
Newcastle to Hexham D 69 2
Newport (IOW) - Branch Lines to A 26 0
Newquay - Branch Lines to C 71 0
Newton Abbot to Plymouth C 60 4
Newtown to Aberystwyth E 41 3
North East German Narrow Gauge D 44 9
Northern France Narrow Gauge C 75 8
North London Line B 94 7
North Woolwich - BLs around C 65 9

O
Ongar - Branch Line to E 05 5
Oswestry - Branch Lines around E 60 4
Oxford to Bletchley D 57 9
Oxford to Moreton-in-Marsh D 15 9

P
Paddington to Ealing C 37 6
Paddington to Princes Risborough C 81 9
Padstow - Branch Line to B 54 1
Peterborough to Kings Lynn E 32 1
Plymouth - BLs around B 98 5
Plymouth to St. Austell C 63 5
Pontypool to Mountain Ash D 65 4
Porthmadog 1954-94 - BL around B 31 2
Portmadoc 1923-46 - BL around B 13 8
Portsmouth to Southampton A 31 4
Portugal Narrow Gauge E 67 3
Potters Bar to Cambridge D 70 8
Princes Risborough - Branch Lines to D 05 0
Princes Risborough to Banbury C 85 7

R
Reading to Basingstoke B 27 5
Reading to Didcot C 79 6
Reading to Guildford A 47 5
Redhill to Ashford A 73 4
Return to Blaenau 1970-82 C 64 2
Rhymney and New Tredegar Lines E 48 2
Rickmansworth to Aylesbury D 61 6
Romania & Bulgaria Narrow Gauge E 23 9
Romneyrail C 32 1
Ross-on-Wye - Branch Lines around E 30 7
Rugby to Birmingham E 37 6
Ryde to Ventnor A 19 2

S
Salisbury to Westbury B 39 8
Saxmundham to Yarmouth C 69 7
Saxony Narrow Gauge D 47 0
Seaton & Sidmouth - Branch Lines to A 95 6
Selsey - Branch Line to A 04 8
Sheerness - Branch Line to B 16 2
Shrewsbury - Branch Line to A 86 4

Shrewsbury to Chester E 70 3
Shrewsbury to Ludlow E 21 5
Shrewsbury to Newtown E 29 1
Sierra Leone Narrow Gauge D 28 9
Sirhowy Valley Line E 12 3
Sittingbourne to Ramsgate A 90 1
Slough to Newbury C 56 7
South African Two-foot gauge E 51 2
Southampton to Bournemouth A 42 0
Southern France Narrow Gauge C 47 5
South London Line B 46 6
Southwold - Branch Line to A 15 4
Spalding - Branch Lines around E 52 9
St Albans to Bedford D 08 1
St. Austell to Penzance C 67 3
Steaming through the Isle of Wight A 56 7
Steaming through West Hants A 69 7
Stourbridge to Wolverhampton E 16 1
St. Pancras to Barking D 68 5
St. Pancras to St. Albans C 78 9
Stratford-upon-Avon to Birmingham D 77 7
Stratford-upon-Avon to Cheltenham C 25 3
Surrey Narrow Gauge C 87 1
Sussex Narrow Gauge C 68 0
Swanley to Ashford B 45 9
Swansea to Carmarthen E 59 8
Swindon to Bristol C 96 3
Swindon to Gloucester D 46 3
Swindon to Newport D 30 2
Swiss Narrow Gauge C 94 9

T
Talyllyn - 50 years C 39 0
Taunton to Barnstaple B 60 2
Taunton to Exeter C 82 6
Tavistock to Plymouth B 88 6
Tenterden - Branch Line to A 21 5
Three Bridges to Brighton A 35 2
Tilbury Loop C 86 4
Tiverton - Branch Lines around C 62 8
Tivetshall to Beccles D 41 8
Tonbridge to Hastings A 44 4
Torrington - Branch Lines to B 37 4
Towcester - Branch Lines around E 39 0
Tunbridge Wells - Branch Lines to A 32 1

U
Upwell - Branch Line to B 64 0

V
Victoria to Bromley South A 98 7
Vivarais Revisited E 08 6

W
Wantage - Branch Line to D 25 8
Wareham to Swanage - 50 yrs D 09 8
Waterloo to Windsor A 54 3
Waterloo to Woking A 38 3
Watford to Leighton Buzzard D 45 6
Welshpool to Llanfair E 49 9
Wenford Bridge to Fowey C 09 3
Westbury to Bath B 55 8
Westbury to Taunton C 76 5
West Cornwall Mineral Railways D 48 7
West Croydon to Epsom B 08 4
West German Narrow Gauge D 93 7
West London - Branch Lines of C 50 5
West London Line B 84 8
West Wiltshire - Branch Lines of D 12 8
Weymouth - Branch Lines around A 65 9
Willesden Junction to Richmond B 71 8
Wimbledon to Beckenham C 58 1
Wimbledon to Epsom B 62 6
Wimborne - Branch Lines around A 97 0
Wisbech 1800-1901 C 93 2
Wisbech - Branch Lines around C 01 7
Woking to Alton A 59 8
Woking to Portsmouth A 25 3
Woking to Southampton A 55 0
Wolverhampton to Shrewsbury E 44 4
Worcester to Birmingham D 97 5
Worcester to Hereford D 38 8
Worthing to Chichester A 06 2

Y
Yeovil - 50 yrs change C 38 3
Yeovil to Dorchester A 76 5
Yeovil to Exeter A 91 8